MW01228199

"Brandon is a man with high ambitions. It is always inspiring to hear his story and to gain insight from his journey."

**—Brandon Patterson, President Jimmy Carter's Former Pastor**

"We first heard about Brandon Gosselin's remarkable story several years ago while working on our book *American Spirit*. We were impressed then, and continue to be now, by his amazing charity, sense of purpose and drive. *My Path to the Presidency: An Action Plan to Realizing YOUR Aspirations* combines those qualities and helps the reader develop a path to their own success. Integrating advice from a wide range of people—Ralph Waldo Emerson to current football heroes—it's sure to influence a future president, indeed."

**—Jim DeFelice and Taya Kyle, New York Times bestselling authors**

"Not many people Brandon's age have realized major aspirations! Even fewer are passionate about sharing what they've learned—and how they've learned it, identifying books and personalities that helped them along the way. Amazing story and tremendous tool!"

**—Tom Ziglar, CEO Zig Ziglar Corporation**

"From the moment that I met Brandon he's had a huge impact on my success. From sharing his network to business advice, I couldn't ask for a better associate. I've never met anyone so willing to help and not expect anything in return. Brandon is definitely one of a kind."

**—Trevor Booker, 8-year NBA veteran turned entrepreneur/business mogul**

"Few moments in your life do you get the opportunity to get your hands on something like this . . . don't put it down. Brandon is the voice that this generation has been waiting (and needing) to hear. Forget motivational fluff, his message comes from practicality, credibility, and truth.

**—Caleb Maddix, *Forbes* 30 Under 30,
Co-Founder of Apex 4 Kids**

# MY PATH TO THE PRESIDENCY

## An Action Plan to Realizing YOUR Aspirations

BRANDON M. GOSSELIN

JONES MEDIA
PUBLISHING

MY PATH to the PRESIDENCY An Action Plan to Realizing YOUR Aspirations
Copyright © 2020 by Brandon M. Gosselin

All rights reserved. No part of this publication may be reproduced, distributed, or
transmitted in any form or by any means, including photocopying, recording, or
other electronic or mechanical methods, without the prior written permission of
the author, except in the case of brief quotations embodied in critical reviews and
certain other noncommercial uses permitted by copyright law.

Jones Media Publishing
10645 N. Tatum Blvd. Ste. 200-166
Phoenix, AZ 85028
www.JonesMediaPublishing.com

Disclaimer:

The author strives to be as accurate and complete as possible in the creation of
this book, notwithstanding the fact that the author does not warrant or represent
at any time that the contents within are accurate due to the rapidly changing
nature of the Internet.

While all attempts have been made to verify information provided in this
publication, the Author and the Publisher assume no responsibility and are
not liable for errors, omissions, or contrary interpretation of the subject matter
herein. The Author and Publisher hereby disclaim any liability, loss or damage
incurred as a result of the application and utilization, whether directly or
indirectly, of any information, suggestion, advice, or procedure in this book. Any
perceived slights of specific persons, peoples, or organizations are unintentional.

In practical advice books, like anything else in life, there are no guarantees of
income made. Readers are cautioned to rely on their own judgment about their
individual circumstances to act accordingly. Readers are responsible for their
own actions, choices, and results. This book is not intended for use as a source
of legal, business, accounting or financial advice. All readers are advised to seek
the services of competent professionals in legal, business, accounting, and finance
field.

Printed in the United States of America

ISBN: 978-1-948382-13-7 paperback
JMP2020.5

# DEDICATION

*To my mom and dad.*

*Growing up was not perfect, and even today, it still is not.*

*But that is what made me who I am today.*

*You are strength. You are perseverance. You are love.*

*Thank you for being the best parents I could ever have asked for.*

Getting to where you need to go isn't a matter of transportation. Sometimes the hand up isn't one that comes on wings or wheels.

— Jim DeFelice & Taya Kyle,
*American Spirit*

Sometimes, the hand up I need is ME.

—All of Us

# CONTENTS

**PART 3**
**Bound for Glory and Service: Building YOUR Aspirations**

**PART 4**
**1600 Penn Avenue: Molding YOUR Aspirations**

**PART 5**
**Path to The Presidency: Achieving YOUR Aspirations**

# FOREWORD

It is my honor to write the foreword for a future president of the Unite States. Yes, you read that right: from White House intern to sitting behind the desk in the Oval Office in 2032, allow me to share a little about my friend Brandon Gosselin and his new book *My Path to the Presidency: An Action Plan to Realizing YOUR Aspirations.*

It was late summer of 2016, and I received a phone call from a long-time friend and well-known real estate investor Robyn Thompson. Robyn mentioned she had a young and driven red-headed intern who had read a few of my books and wanted to meet me. Being someone who enjoys investing in humanity, especially our youth, we set up a date for her intern to visit South Florida.

It was another sunny day in Delray Beach. Ahead of schedule and ten minutes before our meeting, Brandon Gosselin (Robyn's intern) walked up the steep ladder staircase to my oceanfront treehouse office overlooking the Atlantic. Finishing up some work, I asked Brandon to sit down. At first glance, Brandon looked very sharp in his jet-black suit and red tie. With yellow notepad in hand, he sat down. We began our meeting at 1:00 p.m. sharp, as scheduled.

Our conversation started off just like any other. Brandon was respectful, cordial, professional, and to the point (which I like in a meeting). He was curious how I started a real estate career without any formal academic education, beginning with a $50,000 fixer-upper at age twenty-three, then working my way up to building a $50 million, 32,000 sq. ft. direct oceanfront spec home (built without a buyer). We discussed how many of the answers Brandon was seeking could be found in some of my international bestselling books, from *Make it Big to Burst This*! to *Frank McKinney's Maverick Approach to Real Estate Success*. During the hour-long meeting Brandon was asking the right questions and patiently taking notes. I could tell he understood the importance of fast-track learning via other's experiences.

It was my turn to learn more about Brandon that day in my treehouse office. He would share how he had exceptional achievements from being one of the top 300 public speakers in the world through an international competition to being named one of the Top 12 freshman at the University of Oklahoma (Brandon was in the summer leading to his junior year of college at the time). For anyone, let alone a young man his age, what I was absorbing was impressive!

Although exceptional, these accomplishments were not what I was impressed with. As I continued to learn about what made Brandon special, I discovered he had incredibly humble beginnings and overcame an accident where he was pronounced dead only three years before our meeting. You will know more of his story in this book, so I won't ruin it. Keep reading!

Although the meeting started like any other, it did not finish like any other. Brandon's story and his drive to serve others left an impression on me. So much so that before he left our meeting, he asked me to be his mentor, and to this day, Brandon continues to inspire me and so many others.

Anytime I have an event—whether it be for revealing one of my oceanfront masterpieces or a fundraising event for our Caring House Project Foundation (chpf.org)—Brandon is always quick to text me and ask if he can help. Even if he were in

Tennessee, he would fly to Florida in the morning, work our event that night, and leave the next morning to get back for school.

Brandon understands what it takes to be successful. He applies what I refer to as "relentless forward motion." Brandon surrounds himself with the right people and mentors. More importantly, he has Faith and relationship with God that is extremely important to him, and to me too.

As our relationship developed, I began to learn more about Brandon's aspirations. It is excellent to aspire, but as you will learn in this book, Brandon has developed an Action Plan for you. This same Action Plan that has helped him accomplish some of his aspirations, whether it was graduating *summa cum laude* as a college athlete or building a company to a value of $10 million from scratch, Brandon's Action Plan is something you can implement RIGHT NOW. As I mentioned in the opening paragraph, one of his aspirations that I know he will achieve is becoming president of the United States in 2032—he will have my vote!

Brandon's Action Plan was developed from his own personal experiences of trial and error, as well as the mentorship of hundreds of hours spent with high-level mentors. His mentors range from a former national political director for a president of the United States to a former chairman of a Fortune 500 company. Brandon has traveled over 100,000 miles to meet with his mentors, even if a ten-hour drive would only get him thirty minutes with the person he sought.

Without a doubt I know that the lessons, strategies, philosophies, and stories in *My Path to the Presidency: An Action Plan to Realizing YOUR Aspirations* will help you achieve your aspirations. Whether you want to run a million-dollar company, become an elite athlete, be a great professional, or simply be the best person you can be, the Action Plan in this book will help you achieve the success you desire. And, like Brandon, I hope your success will blaze a path for others who seek to learn how to achieve their aspirations in every area of life—even if that desire is to become the president of the United States!

Frank McKinney
7-Time Best Selling Author,
Philanthro-Capitalist & Real Estate Artist
frank-mckinney.com
theaspirebook.com

# INTRODUCTION

Life is not hard!

I want to repeat this, so if there is only one thing you remember from this book, it is the fact that

Life is NOT hard!

Ever since my life-threatening accident in 2013 where I was pronounced dead, I began to create mild success in my life. Whether it was being named as one of the top 300 public speakers in the world by Toastmasters International (a world-wide communication/leadership building organization) in 2016 or interning at the White House in 2017, I was making progress. Friends, family, and my audiences had urged me to write a book. However, I never had the motivation or inspiration to execute on that recommendation.

The final affirmation that led me to write this book was when Jim DeFelice and Taya Kyle featured me in their book called *American Spirit* (2019). *American Spirit* profiles more than thirty individuals, young and old, rich and not-so rich, famous and unknown, who have overcome hardship and done extraordinary things for their communities and the nation at large. Being featured in a book along with some of the great names like David Goggins, who is a former Navy SEAL (ultramarathon runner, ultradistance cyclist, triathlete, motivational speaker, and author), is extremely humbling.

I want to be clear here. This book is **not to impress you**. This book is to **impress upon you** a perspective of life that is personal to me yet universal for anyone to implement in their life. I have shared the speaking stage with notable speakers—such as NFL legend Peyton Manning— spreading my message. I am incredibly passionate about serving others and helping them realize their potential in Achieving their Aspirations!

In reading this book, you will gain simple tips and strategies to help you achieve your Aspirations. I cannot recall the author, but I came across this quote a couple years ago:

"There is NO ONE KEY TO SUCCESS. There are many different strategies to find your success. You just have to find the one that works best for you."

With that said, this book is not a be-all and end-all book that gives you the easy cut strategy. I simply share a few tips and strategies I have personally learned from experience or learned from my mentors, mentors who have ranged from the richest man in Alabama—Jimmy Rane—to my Oklahoma Basketball Hall of Fame high-school basketball coach—Coach Randy Turney.

So, let's start your Path. Let's begin your Path to **Understanding** who you are and using that information in **Designing** your Aspirations in life. As we are **Building** your Aspirations, we are going to learn the importance of **Molding** your Aspirations and improving your Path. Finally, as we aspire together, we will strive to **Achieve** your Aspirations! After each chapter, there will be an action step to assist you in this process. BUT before we do that, let's go back to . . .

## LIFE IS NOT HARD!

*You can also find the free *Path to the Presidency Workbook* to finish all the action steps at www.PathToThePresidency.com.

Don't get me wrong: life is challenging. I say life is NOT "hard" because of the word "hard." Allow me to explain:

Society has shaped our unconscious mind, the reservoir of feelings, thoughts, urges, and memories that are out of our conscious awareness but affect our day-to-day behavior. When we hear the word "hard," our unconscious mind already triggers in our brain the thoughts, "I guess I *can't* do it . . . Who am I to think I can . . .?"

You may disagree with this, and that is okay. However, I do encourage you to try an exercise. Replace the word "hard" with the word "challenging." This simple change of words will have a profound impact on the way you see your life.

As human beings, we have some degree of a competitive personality. When we hear a task, assignment, or job is "challenging," our unconscious mind automatically puts a fire in us and an attitude that says, "GAME ON!"

Every time you are about to say something is "hard," I encourage you instead to say that something is "challenging." You may or may not see an immediate change in the way you approach that "challenging" task in your life; however, your unconscious mind will begin to lead you on the right Path to your Aspirations. This Path will lead you to accomplish things your friends, family, and even yourself never thought possible.

Let's turn the page. We are on Your Path together.

## PART 1

# Deer Diary:
# Understanding You

# CHAPTER 1

# **Broken**

It's not about the destination;
it's about the journey.

—Ralph Waldo Emerson

From losing his father at a young age to losing his young wife to tuberculosis when he was twenty-six, Ralph Waldo Emerson had a perspective on life that allowed him to become one of the most prolific thinkers in history.

Trained as a minister, Ralph attended both Harvard University and Harvard School of Ministry. Ralph made a majority of his money from giving lectures on the literary works he produced. His first secular publication was called *Nature*, which was the launching point of his literary career. Emerson made an effort to surround himself with thinkers and intellects.

Keeping a journal most of his life, Ralph wrote on October 25, 1820:

I find myself often idle, vagrant, stupid, and hollow. This is somewhat appalling and, if I do not discipline myself with diligent care, I shall suffer severely from remorse and the sense of inferiority hereafter. All around me are industrious (students) and they shall be great, I am indolent and shall be insignificant . . .

## MY STORY

I grew up as the youngest child in a one-bedroom house of six people. Being the first in my family to graduate from a four-year university was the dream. On May 16, 2013, my dream seemed to be within reach as I had graduated valedictorian of my high-school senior class. I was also lucky enough to be recognized as one of the top ten Class B basketball players in the state of Oklahoma. However, just nine days later, on May 25, 2013, I was pronounced dead.

May 25 was like any other night for my friends and me in our small town of Burlington, Oklahoma—a town of 150 people. We were riding four-wheelers, camping out, and playing basketball on a tattered, abandoned basketball court about twelve miles away from our campsite. We were zooming through the night on our four-wheelers. The warm summer air was blowing through my hair and the stars, moon, and dinky four-wheeler headlight was illuminating our way. Then out of nowhere, it happened.

Going fifty-five miles per hour at 11:30 at night, not wearing a helmet, and only wearing shorts and a "bro tank," we collided head-on with a deer. My two underclassman friends were riding the four-wheeler with me. They were quickly ejected from the four-wheeler seat, landing in the grassy ditch. However, I would get the worst of it.

I went over the handlebars and came in contact with the pavement of the road headfirst. To make a long story short, I woke up in the hospital nine days later to discover what had happened. I woke up with a third-grade mental capacity and hardly had the ability to walk. I busted the left side of my face wide open, almost losing my left eye. A blood vessel burst in my brain by my basal ganglia and I received second and third degree burns all over my body from scraping against the concrete. After about a month in the hospital, I was finally released to go home.

---

Side Note: Maybe you can identify with Ralph Waldo Emerson's excerpt from October 25, 1820. Do you feel surrounded by people who are doing incredible things? At times do you feel inferior, idle, and even stupid? . . . I know I have been there, and sometimes if I am not careful, I find myself going back there.

---

In this book, we will be focusing on Understanding, Designing, Building, Molding, and Achieving your Aspirations along your Path.

We will discuss how to understand who you are and why you think, act, and do what you do. We will discuss how to design your Path to achieve your Aspirations. We will explore how to build upon your foundation to give you a solid Path. We will uncover how to be agile and mold your Aspirations as you, your surroundings, and your environment changes. At the end of this book, you will be equipped with a solid Path to achieve your Aspirations.

Not sure what an Aspirations is? Don't worry; you will learn that in chapter 5. Keep on reading; our journey has just begun!

# ACTION STEP 1

Write down the greatest obstacle you have had to overcome. List who and what helped strengthen you during this time. Then list who and what hindered you during this time.

## Greatest obstacle

_____

_____

_____

## Who helped and strengthened me?

1) _____

2) _____

3) _____

4) _____

# Who hindered me?

1)
_____

2)
_____

3)
_____

4)
_____

# CHAPTER 2

# When You Realize

When you realize that the people who are changing the world . . . the people who are influencing our society every single day are no smarter than you, then you will realize you can do just the same.

—Steve Jobs

Although it is not well known, Steve Jobs was adopted from birth. His birth mother, Joanne Schieble Simpson, wanted Steve to be college-educated like her and Steve's birth father, Abdulfattah John Jandali. Paul Jobs and Clara Jobs—Steve's adopted parents—were not college educated; however, they promised Joanne and Abdulfattah they would pay for Steve to go to college.

While Clara taught Steve to read and write, his father Paul taught him how to work with his hands. And by the young age of ten, Steve's life of *tinkering* and inventing had begun. At Homestead High School, Steve met Steve Wozniak, who later became the fellow cofounder of Apple.

Steve Jobs would then go to Reed College, where he would shortly drop out. He then traveled to India for enlightenment. Upon his return, he and Steve Wozniak started a group (Homebrew Computer Club) where they would gather with fellow inventors to display and showcase what everyone was developing. Before too long, Apple was born in the garage of Steve Job's parents.

## MY STORY

After a month in the hospital, I was released to go home. Lying in my bed at my parents' home, I was feeling helpless. One month ago, I was "Mr. High School." Now, I was "Mr. Hopeless." I struggled to make sense of everything going on. Besides the distracting smell of my mother burning her blueberry muffins (she makes a good breakfast though), my head was spinning with what my doctors told me . . .

"Brandon, your life is completely changed from here on out. Take it easy."

"Brandon, we are sorry for what happened, but we highly recommend you postpone your endeavors to attend the University of Oklahoma in the fall."

"Brandon, this is your new life . . . learn to deal with it."

Lying there with my world turned upside down and no hope in sight, I gave in. I decided to accept my circumstances. This *was* my new life.

Struggling with negative thoughts that no person should have to deal with, I was trying to find encouragement. I was trying to find hope. I scrolled through Facebook, reading motivational quotes and watching inspirational clips on YouTube. I came across this interview with Steve Jobs, and he essentially said:

"When you realize that the people who are changing the world... the people who are influencing our society every single day are no smarter than you. Then YOU will realize YOU can do just the same."

"Wait . . . me? No smarter than me?" I thought to myself over and over while struggling with the fact that just one month ago, I woke up to a third-grade mental capacity. However, that night I decided I was not going to allow my circumstances to determine who or what I was going to be. I decided that I was going to attend the University of Oklahoma only three short months after being pronounced dead, waking up to a third-grade mental capacity, and hardly having the ability to walk.

The summer between my senior year of high school and my freshman year of college was full of being terrified of going out in public—especially to the local Walmart. I knew the first thing people noticed was the big gash on the side of my face.

Simple tasks like walking up and down the stairs to the basement of our house were challenging. Every day I strived to get better. I practiced Lumosity Brain Games to improve my mental abilities, ranging from math to cognition and language.

Nonetheless, with a determination to succeed, and despite a reluctant mother who was not ready to send her baby boy to college, I made it to the University of Oklahoma. Shortly after arriving at the University of Oklahoma, I was in a meeting for the President's Leadership Class (PLC)¬.

---

Side Note: In chapters 12, 14, and 18, you will learn the importance of surrounding yourself with incredible people like those I was fortunate enough to have in PLC.

---

In the meeting, we learned about U-ZOO and Strength Finders 2.0. These were personality quizzes used to help us better understand ourselves and others. I learned what I was good at and why. Just as important, I learned what I was NOT good at and why. My world started to make sense again, and it began to come together. My life seemed to be on the up-and-up. Well, at least that is what it seemed . . .

## ACTION STEP 2

Make a list of 3 strengths and 3 weaknesses you believe you have. Then ask 3 family members and/or close friends what they believe are your 3 strengths and 3 weaknesses. Once you have done this, take 2 personality quizzes. The first is called Strength Finders 2.0 by Gallup ($20). If you are unable to afford Gallup's version, take the 16 Personality Test by Briggs Myers (free). At the end, each test will explain what you can do with what you have learned.

### What I believe are my 3 strengths

1) _____

2) _____

3) _____

### What I believe are my 3 weaknesses

1) _____

2) _____

3) _____

## What my family and friends think are my 3 strengths

1) _____

2) _____

3) _____

## What my family and friends think are my 3 weaknesses

1) _____

2) _____

3) _____

## My top 5 strengths according to Strength Finders 2.0 (top 1–5)

1) _____

2) _____

3) _____

4) _____

5) _____

## My top 5 weaknesses according to Strength Finders 2.0 (bottom 30–34)

1) _____

2) _____

3) _____

4) _____

5) _____

**What is my personality according to the 16 Personalities Test?**

_____

_____

_____

**Who are 3 famous people with the same personality?**

1) _____

2) _____

3) _____

# CHAPTER 3

# **Define Your Success**

The difference between successful people
and others is how long they spend time
feeling sorry for themselves.

—Barbara Corcoran


Growing up as the second oldest of ten children, Barbara Corcoran was part of a large family with unstable income. Barbara was known as the "fun" sibling, as she was always in charge of activities to keep her siblings entertained. Barbara made it her job to keep her siblings entertained and distracted from their father, who would regularly talk down to their mother and was emotionally abusive to the family. This abuse fueled Barbara to be unbridled by her gender in New York City—a city dominated by men during the time she began her career—where she became a real estate mogul.

Barbara credits her work ethic to her mother, Florence. It is difficult for Barbara to recall a time when her mother was resting, sleeping, or even lying down to take a break. With her mother taking care of all ten children, Barbara learned tremendous skills in efficiency and diligence.

In her adult life, when she was beginning her real estate career, Barbara's boyfriend (and business partner) broke up with her and decided to marry Barbara's assistant. After one year, Barbara decided to finally end the professional partnership with her ex. Her ex would go on to tell Barbara that "she will never succeed without him." Destined for success, Barbara used that as fuel and credits that statement as one of the best gifts she ever received.

Today, Barbara Corcoran is one of the most influential businesswomen in the world, an author, and a television personality on the hit TV show *Shark Tank*, where entrepreneurs pitch their business ideas to successful business moguls in hope of investment and partnership.

## MY STORY

The night of the accident, before I left my house to go to the campsite, I got into a big fight with my mother. She was badgering me on how I should not go out with my friends and how she thought it was best if I just stayed home. Even though I had gone on these types of outings with my friends numerous times, she said that something just did not feel right. However, fueled with frustration, I was fed up and things escalated.

"I just graduated high school. I am a man now. I can do what I want!" I exclaimed.

Trying to be even-keeled and calm, my mother gathered herself and said, "Sweetie, I know you are a man; I just think it's best you stay home tonight."

But I was not having it. I grabbed the truck keys, continued to yell at my mother, slammed the garage door behind me, yelling, "I am tired of being treated like a little kid, just leave me alone! I wish I did not have to deal with this crap anymore!" I sped out of the driveway and did not look back . . .

That night my mother received a phone call at two o'clock in the morning from our neighbor down the street saying, "Aliene, the boys have been in an accident. They are at the hospital in Wichita. You need to get there quick; Brandon may not make it!"

With tears in her eyes, she franticly woke up my father, who was next to her, to break the news. They quickly got dressed, jumped into my Dodge Challenger, and made an hour-and-fifteen-minute drive in about forty minutes. (He smoked in my car. The two rules I had was no food or drinks in the car and NO SMOKING. He did both . . .)

Defining Success

One of the things my mother taught me was how to define success. As a little kid growing up, the media, movies, and top celebrities portrayed what success was. I thought success was having lots of money, being famous, and being able to get any material thing. However, it was not until I was a senior in high school that my mom helped me understand what success truly was. She asked me what success was to me, and I gave her the answer society told me. She then asked if I saw her as successful . .

Feeling like a jerk, I was hesitant to answer. My mom did not have lots of money, was not famous, and could not get any material thing. She looked me in the eyes and said, "Brandon, success is what you determine it to be, not what the world tells you it to be. For me, success was raising you four children, being an incredible wife and mother, and making sure all my children knew how to cook and clean."

Completely surprised, I finally saw my mother as one of the most successful people I knew. She had mastered her "success." With six grandkids, her definition of success has molded into also being the best grandmother she can be—she is incredibly successful at that too.

## ACTION STEP 3

With this understanding of success, write down what you want your success to be. Then, write down characteristics you have to embody to achieve your success.

### What is my definition of success?

_____

_____

_____

### 5 characteristics I must possess to obtain this success

1) _____

2) _____

3) _____

4) _____

5) _____

# CHAPTER 4

# Lead by Leading Yourself

Before you can lead others, You must be
able to lead Yourself.

—John Wooden

Coach Wooden coached basketball legends like Kareem Abdul-Jabbar and led his teams to ten National Collegiate Athletic Association (NCAA) championships in twelve seasons. What made Coach Wooden stand out beyond his unheard-of coaching ability was who he was as a person.

Growing up on a farm in Indiana, John's family life included no electricity, little money, and basketball, which he played with his three brothers.

John grew up to be a true patriot, having served in the Navy as a lieutenant in World War II.

He coached high school and college basketball, where he developed the Pyramid of Success. The Pyramid of Success was John's teaching model that focused on inspiring students and teams to derive the most from their potential. John will forever be remembered as one of the greatest of all times.

Written in the foreword, former head football coach of the 49ers, Bill Walsh, reflects on Coach John Wooden in Coach Wooden's book *Wooden*:

> "John Wooden was a 'philosopher-coach' in the truest sense: a man whose beliefs, teachings, and wisdom go far beyond sports, and ultimately address how to bring out the very best in yourself and others in all areas of life."

## MY STORY

The first semester of my freshman year at the University of Oklahoma was off to a great start! I was learning more about myself, Understanding my personality, and making great friends. College seemed to be going great . . . at least that is what I thought.

Midterms of my freshman year rolled around, and to my astonishment, I was failing my classes. Please understand that this was a wakeup call for me. "Failing?" I asked myself. "At no point in my life have I ever failed a class, let alone gotten a B, and all of a sudden, I'm failing?"

After doing more research, I learned exactly what had happened the night of my accident. The blood vessel that burst in my brain the night of my accident was right by my basal ganglia. Your basal ganglia controls four main things in your life: (1) your voluntary movement, (2) your cognitive capacity, (3) your learning capabilities, and (4) your . . . uhhh . . . oh yeah, your memory!

Practically everything that we use to function in day-to-day life was hit for me—I basically had a "new brain." I had to relearn how to think. I had to relearn how to memorize. I had to relearn how to learn. I had to adapt to my "new brain." Thus, I began the journey of leading myself.

Every morning I would go to the gym for one hour—a healthy body is a healthy brain. Every morning after the gym I would have a quiet time and do a Bible study—a healthy spirit is a healthy brain. Every day I would eat greens and other healthy foods—what fuels your body fuels your brain. Every day I would go to tutors to help me better understand the material I was learning in class. I also began to do self-studies to understand how my "new brain" worked, learned, memorized, and processed material. Every evening I would schedule my next day so that I could optimize every minute. I became the master of my life, and I began to take the lead. However, staying motivated and staying inspired was a challenge.

Side Note: If you miss your morning routine or are not able to do everything in it, it is okay. Of course, do not make a habit of missing or not completing your morning routine, but also do not let missing or not completing your morning routine ruin your day either.

Look at it this way. If you had $86,400 in a piggy bank and someone came and stole $2,700 from you, would you throw away the other $83,700? No way! Right? Well, do not do that with your day either. We are all given the same 86,400 seconds in a day. It's how we choose to use it that truly matters.

## ACTION STEP 4

Create a morning routine. Answer questions like: What time am I waking up? What are the first three things I will do before I scroll through social media (this is a big one)? Am I going to take a cold shower every morning to get my blood flowing? (Google benefits of cold showers.) Am I going to drink a full glass of room temperature water within thirty minutes after I wake up? How long am I setting aside to think, meditate, or pray? How long will I exercise? What will I do to exercise?

Be specific and stick to it. It is okay if you mess up your morning routine, just keep working on making your morning routine a habit.

**What time am I going to bed?**

_____

_____

**What time am I waking up?**

_____

_____

## What are the first 3 things I will do before I scroll through social media?

1) _____

2) _____

3) _____

## How long will I think, meditate, or pray?

_____

_____

## How long will I exercise?

_____

_____

## What will I do for exercise?

_____

_____

## 3 books I can read for a total of at least 30 minutes

1) _____

2) _____

3) _____

## What 3 affirmations will I say in the mirror out loud to myself? (See ch. 18)

1) _____

2) _____

3) _____

# CHAPTER 5

# Motivation, Inspiration & Aspiration

Motivation is momentary. Inspiration
is temporary. Aspirations are perpetual.
Aspirations take you from who you are
today to who you will become tomorrow.

—Frank McKinney

A true modern-day Renaissance man, Frank McKinney is a 7x Best-Selling Author (in five genres), ultramarathon runner, aspirational speaker, and a world-renowned philanthro-capitalist (he builds oceanfront property for the ultrawealthy in South Florida and with that money has established twenty-nine self-sufficient villages in the country of Haiti).

Upon attending his fourth high school in four years (the other three high schools "asked him" to leave), Mr. McKinney earned his high school diploma with a 1.8 GPA. Then, with $50 in his pocket and without the benefit of further education, Mr. McKinney left his native state of Indiana for Florida, in search of his life's highest calling.

Not only is he a phenomenal businessman and real estate artist, but Mr. McKinney is also an incredible husband and father. Mr. McKinney walked his daughter Laura to school for the first fourteen years of her life. He has a genuine heart to serve others. Mr. McKinney is a respected leader in South Florida, Haiti, and the world.

## MY STORY

Although I was taking lead of my life, I would feel in the dumps and completely unmotivated at times. No matter how much I wanted to do something, my inspiration would flee me. Nonetheless, I was determined to defy the odds and be the best person I could be for my family.

Through exceptional work ethic, determination, and incredible support from friends and family, I was able to go from failing at midterms during my first semester of freshman year at the University of Oklahoma to finishing the semester with a 4.0 GPA.

My life was improving on all levels. I was slowly Achieving my goals and striving to overcome the side effects from the accident I had only six months prior. Feeling blessed, I was going into the spring semester of my freshman year. Little did I know I had something in store for me, unlike anything I had ever faced . . .

\* \* \*

Two years later, in the summer of 2016, I learned why my motivation and inspiration would flee:

I found myself sitting in Frank McKinney's treehouse office overlooking the Atlantic Ocean. Mr. McKinney looked at me and asked, "Brandon, do you know the difference in motivation, inspiration, and Aspiration?"

Thinking this was a trick question, I looked at him and said, "They are essentially the same thing?"

With a big smile on his face and a deep breath of the salty ocean air, he looked at me and explained, "Motivation is momentary and lasts about a day. You grew up in the country? You worked on a farm?" he asked me.

"Of course, some days we were working twelve-to-fifteen-hour days," I replied.

He went on, "At the end of a gruesome day's work, you go and take a shower. You stand there and watch all your sweat and dirt from the day wash down the drain. There, too, you will find your motivation washing down. Motivation is momentary."

He continued, "Inspiration, however, is temporary and lasts about as long as a bad sunburn." Once again, Mr. McKinney looked at me and said with a smirk, "Brandon, do you ever get sunburned?"

I chuckled under my breath. I responded, "Mr. McKinney, I'm a ginger. I have red hair and freckles. I'm in the sun for thirty minutes and I turn as red as a tomato."

Laughing, he replied, "Inspiration lasts about as long as a bad sunburn. You have it for maybe four to six days, and before you know it, your sunburn is gone—along with your inspiration."

Now he has me curious, "Mr. McKinney, so how is Aspiration different?"

As he looked at his six Badwater race medals with a big smile (the world's most challenging footrace at 120 miles in 118-degree weather, and an Aspiration of his), he enlightened me: "An Aspiration is perpetual, and it is DNA-altering, Brandon. In the times you want to give up and quit, the times where life seems to be too much, you remember your Aspirations. Your Aspirations perpetuates you. Discover your Aspirations, and you have the ability to not only positively change your life, but the lives of those around you."

---

Side Note: You can have more than one Aspiration. Aspirations can be professional, spiritual, or personal. As you will see, your Aspirations will align with your definition of success.

---

## ACTION STEP 5

Now that you understand the difference between motivation, inspiration, and Aspiration (M.I.A.), write a social media post, blog, or something that you can share with your family and friends. Make sure to illustrate the difference in M.I.A. Mental health is extremely important, not only for yourself but to those around you.

**What my Facebook/Instagram post will say**

_____

_____

_____

_____

_____

**What picture I will use**

_____

_____

## What my tweet will say

_____

_____

## Which friends I will tag

_____

_____

(BONUS ACTION: In your social media post, tag me so I can follow you!)

## PART 2

# Make a Difference: Designing Your Aspirations

# CHAPTER 6

# The Thief in the Night

Be thankful for what you have; you'll end
up having more. If you concentrate on
what you don't have, you will never, ever
have enough.

—Oprah Winfrey

Oprah grew up in rural Mississippi with a very strict and sometimes abusive grandmother. Oprah was extremely poor and would often wear potato sacks as clothing. Although strict, her grandmother was an encourager and taught Oprah how to read. At the age of thirteen, Oprah experienced sexual trauma from members of her family and would soon run away from home to escape all of her abuse. At fourteen years old, she became pregnant and prematurely gave birth to a baby boy who would shortly pass away.

From a young age, Oprah was incredibly intelligent and was quickly recognized for her talents. She was granted a scholarship through the Upward Bound program to go to school in an affluent community. (The Upward Bound program provides opportunities for participants to succeed in their precollege performance and ultimately in their higher education pursuits.)

A remarkable woman, Oprah understood she had to have a willingness to see each moment for what it was, accept it, forgive the past, take responsibility, and move forward: a mantra she lives throughout her life. She became one of the most influential, self-made female billionaires and has inspired many to realize that where you come from does not determine who you are and who you are going to be.

## MY STORY

Suicide is never a joking matter. It can happen to the best of us. Its grip knows no age, no race, no religion, no creed, and no gender. It is a thief in the night that can take someone you love or a stranger you have never met, and it may have even attempted to take you.

During the second semester of my freshman year, another side-effect of my Traumatic Brain Injury (TBI) began to take full effect. (It's good to point out that a common side effect of a TBI is emotional instability and, if not monitored, it can have severe side effects.) I was pushing myself day in, day out. I was pushing myself with high expectations and lofty goals. Little did I know, my emotional instability had me on the brink of destruction.

I remember it like it was yesterday. At two o'clock in the morning I was sitting in the common area of the Couch Center Residence Hall where I was living. Emptied from a busy day, I was drained emotionally, physically, spiritually, and mentally. I felt like crap. My mind was in a place where a mind should never go. A place it had been when I was released to go home from the hospital (chapter 2), but far fiercer. It was simple: I could leave the stress and pain. I could leave my problems of not thinking I'm good enough. I could leave the thoughts of never reaching my goals.

I was in the middle of writing *the letter* when the words "self-compassion" came into my head. Being the millennial I am and admittedly not the most clever with words, I quickly turned to Google and typed in "What is 'self-compassion'?" It read: "Being Understanding of yourself when you fail, feel inadequate, and hopeless. Understanding that you are not the only one that suffers from these feelings and that you are not alone. Being content with what you have, but striving for a better tomorrow." By the grace of God, I put down that pen, tore the piece of paper, and began to weep.

---

Side Note: Self-compassion is not a weakness but a strength. Self-compassion is humility, not feebleness. Self-compassion is Understanding you are not alone. Self-compassion helped me overcome and manage the emotional instability I had from my TBI.

---

During this time, I reached out to spiritual mentors and psychologists to help me manage and understand my emotions. I went to counseling. I took control of my emotions and learned how to manage them. To this day, I have helped many of my friends overcome a similar *letter* moment.

A common misconception is that going to see a counselor or having a psychiatrist is a sign of weakness and being crazy. However, I propose quite the opposite. For example, LeBron James is one of the most amazing athletes in the world. How did he become that way? He had coaches and trainers teach him how to train his muscles. They gave him drills and exercises to condition his muscles to perform at peak capacity. If LeBron got injured, his coaches and trainers taught him how to improve and come back stronger.

Much like your muscles, your brain has the ability to be trained, exercised, and improved. "How do I do this?" you may ask. Simple. Go to a counselor. Talk to a psychiatrist. You going to a counselor to improve your brain, emotions, etc. is no different than Lebron James having coaches train him to be an elite athlete.

Most of us probably heard the phrase "Be Like Mike" or saw the iconic '90s "Be Like Mike" Gatorade commercial that featured Michael Jordan (quite possibly the greatest professional basketball player ever). The phrase "Be Like Mike" meant to be a successful basketball player who seemed to have it all and made it look easy. Just as Lebron and Michael trained their muscles to have elite athletic abilities, maybe we should "Be Like Mike" and train our brains to have elite minds.

## ACTION STEP 6

Make a list of 5 people you are grateful for. Make a list of 5 experiences, objects, or things you are thankful for. HANDWRITE a letter to each of the 5 people on your list, letting them know you are grateful for them and why you are grateful for them. Either hand deliver or mail the handwritten letter to them.

### 5 people I am grateful for

1) _____

2) _____

3) _____

4) _____

5) _____

### Why I am grateful for these 5 people

1) _____

2) _____

3) _____

4) _____

5) _____

## 5 experiences/objects/things I am grateful for

1) _____

2) _____

3) _____

4) _____

5) _____

# CHAPTER 7

# See Your Future,
# Be Your Future

See your future. Be your future.

—Ty Webb

Ty Webb is a fictional character from the 1980s comedy *Caddyshack* played by Chevy Chase. Ty is an eccentric businessman who is pretty laid back and great at golf. Ty spends a good portion of the movie with his caddy, Danny. Danny is unsure of what he wants to do with his life after high school. He was being pressured by his dad to go to college, while he was not sure what he wanted to do.

Ty promises Danny that it is okay to not be sure about college (a statement that is true today for anyone struggling with that same thought). Ty essentially said that it is okay that Danny did not know what he wanted in life, he would one day would figure it out.

---

Side Note: The plot of the movie is quite interesting. Set aside the crude humor it has at times, there is much to be learned from the film. In fact, like many movies and TV shows—if you look at them through the right lens—you can find valuable lessons . . . Although some may take more looking than others.

---

## MY STORY

Complete transparency here . . . Growing up, my father was a jerk. He was emotionally and physically abusive to my mother, siblings, and me. Later in life, I came to understand that he simply was just learning how to cope with running his own business and feeding a family of six. Over the years, he has matured a remarkable amount—he is now an incredible father, a much, much better husband, and an amazing grandfather.

If there is a phrase I remember my dad always saying, it was, "See your future. Be your future." My dad was a passionate man that was continuously pursuing the next thing. I attest much of my drive and perseverance to him. One day when I was sixteen years old, I was trying to decide what college I wanted to go to when I graduated from high school. Even though neither he nor my mother graduated with a four-year degree, he said, "Brandon, I don't care what you do. I will support you in anything you do. Just do something; you will eventually get to where you want to go. See your future. Be your future."

Funny enough, after he said that, we went down to his man cave and watched Caddy Shack. Lo and behold, I heard Chevy Chase say, "See your future. Be your future." I looked at my father with a big grin. He smiled back and said, "Where do you think he got that quote from?"

By no means was my father perfect growing up. However, finding the silver lining and the good in people is incredibly important. Are there negative things I learned from my father? Yes. Did his parenting influence the man I am today and teach me to set goals? Absolutely. As we grow and mature, it is crucial for us to understand that our upbringing has both negatives and positives. Never sulk in the negative; cherish the positives. Make the most of your relationship now before it is too late.

## ACTION STEP 7

Remember in chapter 3 where you wrote what success is to you? From that statement, what can be an Aspiration to help you achieve that success? (Reread chapter 5 if you need help remembering what an Aspiration is).

With your Aspiration, list 5 short-term goals (0–6 months), 3 medium-term goals (6–24 months), and 1 long-term goal (24+ months). Something to remember when setting goals is to set them APART.

**Achieve:** Your goal is possible and realistic to obtain.

**Precise:** You are detailed about what your goal is. Do not be vague.

**Assess:** You are able to identify an amount, degree, or prestige you want to obtain with your goal.

**Relevant:** Your goal has to be relevant to you and your Aspiration.

**Time Bound:** Set a time frame of when you want to obtain the goal.

All of your goals should be in line with your Aspiration.

(Repeat this Action Step for your other Aspirations)

## My Aspiration:

_____

_____

_____

## My 5 short-term APART goals (identify how they Are APART)*

(0–6 Months)

Short Goal 1)

_____

_____

_____

Short Goal 1 A.)

_____

_____

_____

Short Goal 1 P.)

_____

_____

_____

Short Goal 1 A.)

_____

_____

_____

Short Goal 1 R.)

_____

_____

_____

Short Goal 1 T.)

_____

_____

_____

## My 3 medium-term APART goals (identify how they are APART)*

(6–24 Months)

Medium Goal 1)

_____

_____

_____

Medium Goal 1 A.)

_____

_____

_____

Medium Goal 1 P.)

_____

_____

_____

Medium Goal 1 A.)

_____

_____

_____

Medium Goal 1 R.)

_____

_____

_____

Medium Goal 1 T.)

_____

_____

_____

## My 1 long-term APART goal (identify how it is APART)*

(2+ years)

Long Goal 1)

_____

_____

_____

Long Goal 1 A.)

_____

_____

_____

Long Goal 1 P.)

_____

_____

_____

Long Goal 1 A.)

_____

_____

_____

Long Goal 1 R.)

_____

_____

_____

Long Goal 1 T.)

_____

_____

_____

*You can also find the free *Path to the Presidency Workbook* to finish all the action steps at www.PathToThePresidency.com.

# CHAPTER 8

# Preparing to Fail

By failing to prepare,
you are preparing to fail.

—Benjamin Franklin

The fifteenth of seventeen children, Benjamin Franklin was born in 1708 and is a Founding Father of the United States of America. Only two years of formal schooling growing up, Benjamin Franklin still found himself reading and learning on his own. His love for writing came from working with his older brother in a printing shop. Working around a printing shop while growing up allowed him to better understand literary works, language, and the art of writing.

Benjamin Franklin went on to influence much of what we know today. From the Declaration of

Independence to the United States Constitution, he was an inspiration, a leader, and a faithful servant of the American people. He was also a fashion icon in France, by dressing in his rustic frontiersman with plain clothes and a fur hat. This look would go on to be his "trademark" look, so much so that French women would try to mimic this by having oversized hairdos called "coiffure a la Franklin."

More recently, Benjamin Franklin has influenced tech billionaire and entrepreneur Elon Musk of the electric car company Tesla. Elon, in an interview by Foundation in 2012, said the following:

"You can see how [Franklin] was an entrepreneur. He started from nothing. He was just a runaway kid."

Benjamin Franklin is a testament to show that you, too, can do incredible things, no matter how much "formal education" you have.

## MY STORY

Having heard Benjamin Franklin's quote for the first time during my freshman year at the University of Oklahoma, I made his quote a mantra of mine. Some of my goals I developed and planned to achieve were (1) become a Top 12 Freshman at the University of Oklahoma, (2) graduate college with the highest honors possible, (3) develop a wealth of $1 million by the age of twenty-five, (4) become a World Champion of Public Speaking, and (5) be the best son, brother, uncle, and dad (this one will be in the future) that I can be.

I was blessed enough to be one of the Top 12 Freshman at OU and was able to do this by planning. Not knowing where to begin, I looked at previous winners of the award and saw what they did to achieve this award. Similarities included leadership roles on campus, volunteering, and outstanding performances in academics. With this in mind, I went on to secure leadership roles on campus, volunteer at different organizations on campus and in the community, and make my academics a priority. By the end of freshman year, I was selected for the award.

Side Note: It's important to point out that once you have a strategy and plan that works, you can sometimes use it as a template for other areas with similar goals. With some tweaking to the strategy, I was able to receive Student of the Year at two other different universities I would later attend.

There are some goals you may or may not achieve. Some goals you will exceed. Some goals just need more time. Some goals just need some adjustments. Either way, you must take action.

A close friend recently told me a quote by Arthur Ashe, a successful tennis player:

"One important key to success is self-confidence. An important key to self-confidence is preparation."

## ACTION STEP 8

In each of your goals from chapter 7, write 3 actionable steps you can take to help you achieve each of these goals.

### My 5 short-term APART goals*

(0–6 Months)

### Short Goal 1:

_____

_____

_____

Short Goal 1, Action Step 1:

_____

_____

_____

Short Goal 1, Action Step 2:

_____

_____

_____

Short Goal 1, Action Step 3:

_____

_____

_____

## My 3 medium-term APART goals*

(6–24 Months)

### Medium Goal 1:

_____

_____

_____

Medium Goal 1, Action Step 1:

_____

_____

_____

Medium Goal 1, Action Step 2:

_____

_____

_____

Medium Goal 1, Action Step 3:

_____

_____

_____

# My 1 long-term APART goals

(2+ Years)

## Long Goal 1:

_____

_____

_____

Long Goal 1, Action Step 1:

_____

_____

_____

Long Goal 1, Action Step 2:

_____

_____

_____

Long Goal 1, Action Step 3:

_____

_____

_____

*You can also find the free *Path to the Presidency Workbook* to finish all the action steps at www.PathToThePresidency.com.

# CHAPTER 9

# Living to Serve

Learning to Do, Doing to Learn, Earning to
Live, Living to Serve.

—National FFA Organization moto

The National FFA Organization is a dynamic
youth organization that changes lives and prepares
members for premier leadership, personal growth,
and career success through agriculture education.
Offered in most rural schools and some urban
schools, the FFA (Future Farmers of America)
is an organization that has built influencers in
our nation. From President Jimmy Carter to pop
singer Taylor Swift, the FFA is for anyone eager to
become a leader. Every year students gather and
pack stadiums for both their State Convention and
the National Convention, where the students come
together for celebration, competition, and learning.

After many changes over the years since its inception in 1928, the FFA has helped millions of students develop core values, a strong work ethic, and a drive to serve your fellow man. Currently, with 700,000+ members, every year local FFA chapters (8,612 in total) hold a community service event for their respective community.

These events range from restoring community parks, restocking community food pantries, and planting trees. The goal for this event is to allow its members to partake in the importance of serving and giving back to the community. It also serves as a token, showing the community that their local FFA chapter appreciates the support they have for them and their organization. No matter what their members choose to do in life, the National FFA Organization encourages to always serve and do your part.

## MY STORY

As a former member of the National FFA Organization myself, I can attest to the positive impact it had on not only me and fellow students but also the community. The Burlington FFA chapter typically has around 35+ students (average chapter size in the U.S. is 75) and is a nationally recognized chapter. A big reason our small chapter was so successful was through the leadership of our former agriculture advisor, Mr. Travis Bradshaw.

Mr. Bradshaw went beyond the duties of a teacher and agriculture-education advisor. He would spend countless hours staying up with this student—sometimes up to three in the morning—making sure they were prepared for a competition the next day. He would teach us how to think creatively and for ourselves.

During my senior year of high school, Mr. Bradshaw asked me to compete in the extemporaneous public-speaking contest. I was given twelve agriculture topics, and I would select one of the topics to prepare a four-to-six-minute speech. The catch? I was only given a thirty-minute window to do this. This competition was my first extemporaneous speaking competition, so I was nervous. I went in, gave my speech with confidence, and finished in third place! Not bad for the first time . . . Sadly, I only gave a one minute, twenty-three second speech, and there were only two other competitors in this competition. Mr. Bradshaw looked at me and said, "Brandon, maybe public speaking just isn't your thing."

---

Side Note: Whether you are still in school or the professional world, reach out to some of your old teachers and professors, and thank them for the impact they had on your life.

---

## ACTION STEP 9

Research 2 volunteer activities you can participate in at least once a month. Contact the organizations and become a consistent volunteer.

### First Volunteer Activity

_____

What is the organization?

_____

How can I serve this organization?

_____

Organization leader(s):

_____

Organization contact info:

_____

How often and when will I serve?

_____

## Second Volunteer Activity

---

What is the organization?

---

How I can serve this organization?

---

Organization leader(s):

---

Organization contact info:

---

How often and when will I serve?

---

# CHAPTER 10

# Mentor Up

Make a list of the people you admire and what makes them amazing. Then go out and become those things yourself.

—Tai Lopez

Tai Lopez was born in Long Beach, California. Since his father was in prison, Tai Lopez's mother and grandmother raised him. At the age of six, Tai Lopez's entrepreneurial journey began. He started by merely selling cherry tomatoes. Learning he could make more money selling lemonade, Tai quickly jumped on this opportunity and was the first kid in his neighborhood to sell lemonade.

Seeing new opportunities and being the first to jump in is one of the talents helping Tai become a successful multi-millionaire, social media influencer, and mentor to many. Instead of trying to make friends and partaking in gang violence where he grew up, Tai turned to reading books. Even to this day, he claims he reads a book a day.

During the Coronavirus Pandemic of 2020, he and his business partner (who happened to be a former NASA scientist), Alex Mehr, became very successful in buying bankrupt name brands like Pier 1 Imports and Modell's. The plan was to completely revamp the brands' e-commerce, keep a few brick-and-mortar locations, and successfully keep these well-known companies alive.

Tai has experienced homelessness, lived with the Amish, and has felt the tightening grip of failure. Nonetheless, he was determined to be successful. With tens of millions of social media followers and owning multiple million-dollar companies, Tai attributes this success much to his mentors.

Side Note: One of the rules Tai likes to live by is called the Law of 33%. This law states you should spend 33 percent of your time with people less experienced who you mentor, then 33 percent of your time with people on your level who become your friends and peers, and the final 33 percent of your time should be spent with people who are ten times further ahead of you, people who you strive to be mentored by. He says not to be afraid to go to the top.

# MY STORY

While in college, I came across Tai Lopez and saw the emphasis he put on getting mentors. From a small town of 150 in northwest Oklahoma, my mentors seemed to be limited to those in either farming or oil. Having spent five summers working on the farm, I grew to understand the importance of work ethic and patience. Now, I wanted to have more mentors in the business world, as I did not see myself in farming or oil.

With a newfound passion for getting mentors, I spent the next seven years traveling the entire continental United States; seven of those months, I lived out of my car. I would spend every extra dime I had to travel across the country to meet someone, even if it was just for a thirty-minute lunch. My persistence paid off, and now I have the distinct pleasure of being mentored by incredible individuals: from a former national political director for a president of the United States to a former partner of Steve Jobs to my Oklahoma Basketball Hall of Fame high-school basketball coach to many former teachers and professors (especially my English teachers, who helped make this book grammatically correct).

I also found the importance of striving to emulate those I may not have the opportunity to call or meet in person. For example, Tommy Pickles from the children's show Rugrats is someone I have looked up to from a young age. Tommy is brave, an adventure-seeker, and always tries to do what is best for his friends and family. I also look up to President Barack Obama, as I believe he is an incredible family man. Putting politics aside, I believe he is a great husband and outstanding father to his daughters. I strive to be as good of a family man as President Barack Obama. Although I may not be able to be directly mentored by some of these people I look up to and admire, I can still strive to embody some of their characteristics.

## ACTION STEP 10

Remember in chapter 3 where you wrote what characteristics you need to embody to achieve your definition of success? Find 5 people that embody at least one of those characteristics. This can include reaching out to people in your network or outside of your network. Inform them you are reaching out because you are strategizing for your success and having mentors is part of the process. Tell them the characteristics you see in them and ask if they would make themselves available for a one-hour meeting per month for a mentor/mentee session.

In addition, find 2 fictional characters and identify the characteristic you would like to embody. Study them, learn how they demonstrate that characteristic, and make a habit of doing the same.

## 5 people who embody a characteristic I want to obtain*

### 1st person name:

_____

_____

1st person characteristic(s):

_____

_____

1st person contact info:

_____

_____

_____

_____

## 2 fictional characters who embody a characteristic I want to obtain*

### 1st character name:

_____

_____

1st character characteristic(s):

_____

_____

How can I observe them?

_____

_____

_____

_____

*You can also find the free *Path to the Presidency Workbook* to finish all the action steps at www.PathToThePresidency.com.

- 100 -

# Bound for Glory and Service: Building Your Aspirations

CHAPTER 11

# Educate Yourself

Education is our passport to the future,
for tomorrow belongs to the people who
prepare for it today.

—Malcolm X

Malcolm X was an extraordinary figure who was born in Omaha, Nebraska, in 1925 to an outspoken Baptist pastor and a Grenadian-American activist. In 1929 Malcom's home was set on fire. Sadly two years later, his father was found dead. Not too long after, his mother was admitted to a mental health hospital. These troubling circumstances put Malcolm and his seven siblings into the foster system. Nonetheless, Malcolm was able to find solace in his education.

Malcolm was an exceptional student and worked very diligently in his studies. In high school, he told his teacher that he wanted to be a lawyer. In a time propagated with racism and segregation, Malcolm was laughed at by his teacher. His teacher told Malcolm that his goals were unrealistic, and "his kind" could not be lawyers.

His teacher's comments did nothing but fuel Malcolm's passion for being the inspiration that he is today. After moving around more, he was arrested in 1946 and sent to prison for burglary, a circumstance that he would again turn around to benefit him. While in prison, Malcolm read any and every book he could get his hands on.

In 1952 he was released from prison and committed himself to the nation of Islam. After some issues with a leader in the Islam faith, he acquitted himself of the Islam faith. Malcolm was not only a voice for civil rights but a voice for human rights. Prepared to die for his beliefs, Malcolm X motivated people of color to realize their worth. Malcolm—if you agree or disagree with his tactics—is someone we can all learn from. The power of self-education and Understanding one's worth are two pillars Malcolm stood on.

# MY STORY

I believe the higher-education system (college) is a resource that adds much value to society. In contrast, a majority of students do not get their money's worth from their higher education because many believe they are only there for four years to get a piece of paper. I believe that most degrees only show that you can commit to something for four years. However, some professions do benefit you from attending higher education and should require you to go to college to become adequately educated. Some of these include being a doctor (healthcare), lawyer, or teacher because those vocations require certifications and high-level exams to obtain a license. If the traditional higher-education setting does not suit you, go to a vocational-technical school, trade school, or other career-enhancing professional-education career option. The goal is to educate yourself better, and education comes in many different forms.

If you do go to higher education, you will discover that sometimes there is a disconnect between the classroom and the "real world." I was finding great value in my "real world" business experiences and mentorship from successful businesspeople. Still, I was struggling to find the same value from the classroom in higher education. However, I learned how to find the value and my Return On Investment (ROI) for the over $200,000 invested in the two pieces of paper I received from college. I found this value by fully utilizing the resources these universities abundantly offered.

While I received my bachelor's in business administration (management) and master's in business administration (international business)—attending two public and one private university—I learned about the universities' great resources. One of these resources I significantly utilized after my accident was the university's mental health counseling services. Mental health, anxiety, and depression rates in middle-school to college-age students are higher than they have ever been. Many universities offer professional counseling to all of their students. Typically, they come at no extra cost to the students, as student fees you already pay cover the costs.

In addition, many universities have a vast alumni network with hundreds, if not thousands of alums, who are eager to mentor young students of their alma mater. A trip to the university's alumni centers will help you get connected with the right people in the university who typically engage with university alumni.

Many professors (although not all) are masters at the craft they teach. Show your professor you are eager to learn, committed to your education, and willing to do the work to become successful. They will usually put forth the effort to assist you in your Aspirations. Assistance could be a referral to someone in their network, or they may take you under their wing. Whether it was the University of Oklahoma, Freed-Hardeman University, or Florida Atlantic University, I utilized all the resources the university offered (I only listed a few of the hundreds offered). Utilize the university and ALL of the resources (organizations, faculty/staff, alumni, career services, etc.) to get your money's worth.

Side Note: Never discount free education! There is an incredible amount of resources on the internet—especially YouTube, where you can learn entire trades for free. Ask if you can shadow people (watch them work) or be their assistant for little or no money— they like the initiative when you say you will work for free. If you cannot shadow or assist them because their profession does not allow that, ask that person if you can help them move or mow their grass so that you can spend time with them; I have done this many times. Sacrifice pleasure for education. You will not regret it.

## ACTION STEP 11

To achieve your success, you must be educated, whether formally (college or trade school) or informally (mentors, YouTube videos, etc.). Take your goals from chapter 7 and make a timeline. For each goal, write how you can become educated to obtain that goal successfully. Do you need a degree? Do you need mentorship? Can you learn from YouTube? Unsure what education you need? Google it.

For your timeline, start with today's date and put the last date as "Achieved my Aspiration." (This can usually range from five to twenty years depending on where you are in life.)

## My 5 short-term APART goals*
(0–6 Months)
### Short Goal 1)

_____

_____

_____

Is formal education required? If so, what kind?

_____

_____

Who can help mentor me to reach this goal?

_____

_____

What can I do today to begin this goal?

_____

_____

How long should it take me to reach my goal?

_____

_____

What resources found online can I use to educate myself?

_____

_____

## My 3 medium-term APART goals*
(6–24 Months)
## Medium Goal 1)

_____

_____

_____

Is formal education required? If so, what kind?

_____

_____

Who can help mentor me to reach this goal?

_____

_____

What can I do today to begin this goal?

_____

_____

How long should it take me to reach my goal?

_____

_____

What resources found online can I use to educate myself?

_____

_____

# My 1 long-term APART goal*

(2+ years)
## Long Goal 1)

_____

_____

_____

Is formal education required? If so, what kind?

_____

_____

Who can help mentor me to reach this goal?

_____

_____

What can I do today to begin this goal?

_____

_____

How long should it take me to reach my goal?

_____

_____

What resources found online can I use to educate myself?

_____

_____

*You can also find the free *Path to the Presidency Workbook* to finish all the action steps at www.PathToThePresidency.com.

# CHAPTER 12

# Get What You Want

You can have everything in life you want if you will just help enough other people get what they want.

—Zig Ziglar

At ten days old, Zig Ziglar was pronounced dead, and as you could imagine, his mother and grandmother were in tears. However, his grandmother was not about to let this new blessing go that easily. Not accepting Zig's fate, Zig's grandmother picked him up and started speaking life into him. She was not speaking to Zig directly; she was pleading to her Heavenly Father to spare her grandson. With answered prayer, Zig miraculously lived, and the world is a greater place because of him.

Zig's mother was a fighter. She raised twelve children while widowed. She was an extraordinary woman of faith. Baptized at the age of twelve, Zig was not entirely confident with his decision. The rest of his youth, Zig could be found in the church because of the influence of his mother, not necessarily by choice. However, it was not until Zig was forty-five did he truly become a follower of Jesus Christ.

One day after a conversation with his son, Zig committed to living his life on "the straight and narrow." Zig attributes much of his success to not partaking in drinking and smoking. Instead, he focused on participating in service, humility, and optimism—characteristics we can all Aspire to have.

People all over the world recognize Zig Ziglar as one of the most prolific motivational speakers in recent history. An incredible salesman, family man, and example, Zig truly cared for others and understood how to be successful. His secret? He had a servant's heart.

## MY STORY

After I heard Tai Lopez talk about the importance of mentors while in college, I had a passion for surrounding myself with mentors. I remember listening to how Tai found his first business mentor, Mike Stainback: Out of luck and tired of sleeping on a couch, Tai opened up a Yellow Page book (that is a directory of businesses for you young folk) and found a full-page ad for an insurance professional offering his services (Mike Stainback). Tai thought to himself, "If he can afford a full-page ad, he must be doing something right."

Tai showed up to Mike's office in a suit too big for him. He was confident and eager to learn. He walked into the meeting with Mike, looked him straight in the eyes, and said, "I will work for free. I just want to know how to make money." (This is a tactic I have also personally used and recommend, especially when you are young and just getting started).

Impressed with this story, I began to research Mike Stainback. With a great deal of effort, I finally found Mike and reached out to him. I called him up and said, "Mr. Stainback, I have been trying to find you because I have been following one of your previous mentees, Tai Lopez. I live in Oklahoma, but I want to drive to you in North Carolina to meet with you for fifteen minutes. If Tai can be as successful as he is with you as his mentor, I believe it is worth the drive." Mike accepted my request, and I drove the over 1,300-mile trip to his office in North Carolina.

Getting to North Carolina from Oklahoma was not free. I had to sacrifice going out to eat with my friends and eliminate buying nonessential things (a practice I still do to this day).

---

Side Note: You see, sometimes you have to make sacrifices to get what you want. You have to do what other people are not willing to do to have the success tomorrow that other people will not have.

---

I arrived in North Carolina and had my meeting with Mike. Before I left his office, I said, "Mike, it was an honor to meet with you. I can see why Tai has been so successful. If you are available, I would like to continue a mentor/mentee relationship with you. If you need your grass mowed, particular tasks done, or help moving, I will do it for you for free because I know the time spent with you and learning from you is more important than any monetary compensation."

To this day, Mike is not only a mentor but a good friend. I have helped him with million-dollar projects, as he too has helped me with mine. Our relationship has molded from mentorship to friendship to even business partners.

## ACTION STEP 12

Find 5 people in your network and 3 people outside of your network. Tell them you are strategizing for your success, and part of that is helping others achieve their success as well. Ask them what you can do to help them. Spend at most 3 hours per week assisting people in this capacity—be protective of your time.

### 5 people in my network

1) _____

2) _____

3) _____

4) _____

5) _____

# 3 people out of my network

1) _____

2) _____

3) _____

# CHAPTER 13

# Shake It Off

Shake it off and move on.

—Tom Hanks

Shuffled from home to home growing up, Tom Hanks was resilient from a young age. His young nomadic life was because of his parents' divorce. When Tom was five years old, his father was continually trying to find a home for them to live in. At one point, Tom, his father, stepmother, and nine other siblings (five being step-siblings) lived in a small basement flat. However, the uncertainty and constant change in Tom's younger years helped him build the skills of being both flexible and resilient: two commonalities most successful people have mastered.

While in high school and excelling in academics, Tom found his passion for acting and theater. In one of his Oscar acceptance speeches, Tom remembers the impact and influence his high-school drama teacher had on him. After getting married and having two children, Tom dropped out of college and focused on his acting career. Tom did not become a success overnight. He started in minimal TV roles, standup comedy, and lesser-known movies.

Having gotten a divorce from his high-school sweetheart, Tom began to receive counseling to improve his mental health. He would then go on to get remarried and converted to his wife's religion of Greek Orthodox. With perseverance, agility, and optimism, Tom would continue to win four Grammy awards and give us incredible movies such as *Forrest Gump*, *Cast Away* ("Wilson!"), *The Green Mile*, and *Toy Story*.

\* \* \*

During my high-school basketball years, Coach Randy Turney always gave each of his players playbooks. Much like Coach John Wooden, Coach Randy Turney knew basketball was more than just a game and used every moment he had with his players to bring the best out of them on the court, in the classroom, and in life. The playbooks Coach Turney gave us contained not only every offensive formation, defensive formation, and over seventy-five plays but also motivational quotes and leadership stories about how to be a team player. One of the stories I remember in particular was about a farmer who was burying his mule that fell into a water well:

"Once upon a time, there was a farmer who had an old mule. The mule fell into a deep dry well and began to cry loudly. Hearing his mule cry, the farmer came over and assessed the situation. The well was deep, and the mule was heavy. He knew it would be difficult, if not impossible, to lift the animal out.

Because the mule was old and the well was dry, the farmer decided to bury the animal in the well. In this way, he could solve two problems: put the old mule out of his misery and have his well filled.

He called upon his neighbors to help him, and they agreed to help. To work they went. Shovel full of dirt after shovel full of dirt began to fall on the mule's back. The mule became hysterical.

Then all of a sudden an idea came to the mule. Each time the farmers would throw a shovel full of dirt on his back, he could shake it off and step up. Shovel full after shovel full, the mule would "shake it off" and "step up." Now exhausted and dirty, but quite alive, the mule stepped over the top of the well."

## MY STORY

While attending Freed-Hardeman University, I got involved with an international public-speaking and leadership-development organization called Toastmasters International. Knowing public speaking is a skill many people lack (as you saw I did from my story in chapter 9), I made an effort to master it in order to set myself apart from my peers.

---

Side Note: A fact often misstated is that people's fear of public speaking is *greater* than dying. The actual fact is that public speaking is feared *more often* than death (I learned that in a public speaking course at OU).

---

Eager to begin, I researched the closest Toastmasters to where I lived and found a club forty minutes away. Not only was it forty minutes away, but it started at 6:15 in the morning on Tuesday! As a college student who would sometimes study until 1 a.m., waking up at 5 a.m. could sometimes be a challenge. Determined to become a better speaker, I joined the Daybreak

Toastmasters in Jackson, TN—an incredible club with even better-quality people.

After being in the club for a few weeks, I learned of a speech competition where the winner would be dubbed the World Champion of Public Speaking. Having encouragement from my fellow peers in the club, I decided to compete in the international competition. This competition was no small feat, as Toastmasters International includes over 358,000 incredible speakers in 141 countries. Members encompass beginners to people who get paid tens of thousands of dollars to deliver a speech. This competition begins on the club level, then area, then division, then district, and finally the world stage. Only the top two speakers from each competition would advance to the next stage, except for district, where only the winner advanced. Challenge accepted!

I started on the club level, and I competed against some outstanding speakers (including someone later recognized in the World's Top 100 Public Speakers). Having practiced a few times, I gave my speech and placed second. I wanted to place first, but I still advanced to area. At area, the competition included the winners from other clubs in our area. The competition was even more fierce.

I gave my speech and again . . . second. Still not Achieving first, I was able to advance to division.

Division was an even bigger competition with even more elite speakers, as this competition included the top two speakers from the areas that were in our division. Luckily, I had feedback from my previous speeches and practiced more and more. My work paid off, and I placed first! I officially booked a spot in the District 43 speech competition—one of the most competitive in the world. This achievement was huge, as the top speaker from here would go to the world stage to compete against the winners from the other districts across the entire world. I practiced my speech five, six, seven times a day leading up to the competition. I would have friends, family, and professors give me feedback. I was determined to become the World Champion of Public Speaking.

The district competition came, and I was ready! My mom, dad, and aunt even drove 600 miles to watch me compete. I got on stage and delivered my speech better than I have ever practiced before! All the speakers finished, and the judges went back to tally the score. Everyone sat there, anxious for the results. Finally, the judges came back and announced the top three speakers with the first place going to the world stage. The lead judge spoke a bit and then said, "In third place from the Daybreak International Club in Jackson, TN, Brandon Gosselin." Overwhelmed with joy, I got a smile from my family, a hug from my mom, and went to accept my award.

That day I did not get the chance to advance to the international stage to compete for world champion; nevertheless, I realized that placing third put me in the top 300 public speakers in the world. Did I achieve the goal I set out for in chapter 8? No. Was I able to get to the international stage to show the judges I should be the world champion? No. But, I never gave up on speaking. To this day, I get paid thousands of dollars to speak across the country to middle schools, high schools, colleges, and leadership conferences. These opportunities are possible because I shook it off and moved on to become a better speaker.

## ACTION STEP 13

Write down a detailed time you "shook it off" and "stepped up." Remember your feelings, the people who supported you (maybe the same people from chapter 1, take note of this), the people who hindered you (perhaps the same people from chapter 1, take note of this), and why you decided to "shake it off" and to "step up." Write this down.

Action Step 13 is your "Referral Testimony" for you to look back on every time you are put in a difficult situation and want to give up.

### My "shake it off" and "step up" moment

_____

_____

_____

_____

_____

_____

## Feelings I experienced

1) _____

2) _____

3) _____

## People who supported me

1) _____

2) _____

3) _____

## People who hindered me

1) _____

2) _____

3) _____

## Why I decided "shake it off" and "step up" moment

_____

# CHAPTER 14

# Quit Working So Hard

It's not that I'm so smart, it's just that I
stay with problems longer.

—Albert Einstein

E=mc², a formula synonymous with Albert Einstein. The first "scientist celebrity," Albert, was born in Germany in 1879. Although his brilliance was a significant characteristic of his, Albert was someone that would play soccer with kids and sometimes forget where he left his shoes. Albert was an everyday guy; Albert was human.

Albert's life was as unconventional as his theories: from having a baby out of wedlock with one of his fellow physics students to upending over 200 years of scientific thinking when he uncovered the mechanics of gravity. Granted, he said that

Isaac Newton's original thoughts on gravity were approximates. Albert gave us a more exact theory through his theory of general relativity.

Albert gave the world a new way to see heroes. Because of Albert, we have GPS, solar panels, and the digital camera. Albert challenged the status quo and stuck to something until he figured it out. His perseverance led us to discoveries that have forever changed our world. Not bad for an everyday guy.

## MY STORY

One night while living out of my car in the fall of 2017, I had the driver's seat pushed back, steering wheel up, my OU pillow I have had since I was in middle school positioned between my head and the glass window, and my FFA Organization blanket I bought in the eighth grade wrapped over me. Before I went to bed, I watched an interview with Bill Gates (the founder of Microsoft) and Warren Buffet (the greatest stock market mogul of our time).

In this 2017 interview by Charlie Rose (you can find it on YouTube), Charlie is trying to discover what made Bill and Warren so successful. What do they do differently than everyone else? How do they spend their time? After all, they have the same twenty-four hours as everyone else in the world.

Bill and Warren discussed how they spend most of their day thinking, reading, and strategizing. They do not partake in activities unless it keeps them in line with what they want, who they are, and who they want to become. For me, this was an incredible thought process:

**Instead of working tirelessly just to "stay busy for the sake of staying busy," I should**

**focus on spending a majority of my day thinking, reading, and strategizing.**

While picking up this habit, I began to develop a skill in strategizing and planning. I then learned the statistics that only about 10 percent of people are natural leaders and that most people are content to be followers. From personal experience, I know you can grow into a leader, even if you are not necessarily a natural leader.

I remember early in the first semester of seventh grade; I went to the principal's office for probably the thirtieth time that semester for acting up in class. With the principal gone for a meeting, I had to speak with the superintendent. The superintendent, Mr. Elliott, who was a legend in Oklahoma education, sat me down and said, "Brandon, when are you going to stop acting up and start acting like a leader? We all have at least one person that looks up to us. You need to become a leader."

As a seventh grader who was a bully throughout grade school, this was the first time that someone said I had the potential to be a leader. Being a leader is something we can all learn. It begins with a passion to serve people, the willingness to learn, and surrounding yourself with the right influences to guide you in becoming a leader. That day, I decided I was going to try to become a leader and be a better example and influence for my peers.

One of the people that influenced me in becoming a leader was Coach Randy Turney. He quickly helped me overcome my acting out and my troublemaking I was doing in class. In basketball practice, he would put me on the baseline and have me run from end to end on the basketball court every time I acted up in class or made a visit to the principal's office. I not only started to act better in class but lost a lot of weight too (at twelve years old, I was 5'4'' and 200 pounds).

---

Side Note: Later in life, I came across a book called *How to Win Friends and Influence People* by Dale Carnegie (an influential self-help guru). In this book, I learned how to understand people better, improve relationships, win others over, and influence behavior through leadership. I highly recommend it. Did I master this skill in seventh grade? No. Do I have this skill mastered now? No. But like Einstein, I am sticking with it!

---

# ACTION STEP 14

Spend at least 30 minutes in the morning just thinking and strategizing for your goals and Aspirations. Are you on schedule? Do you need to adjust? How can you adjust? Will this adjustment keep you on track?

## Time of day I dedicate to thinking/ strategizing

Morning:
_____

Evening:
_____

## Goals that are off schedule

1) _____

2) _____

3) _____

## Goals I need to adjust

1) _____

2) _____

3) _____

## Strategies to adjust

1) _____

2) _____

3) _____

## One thing I want to accomplish today

1) _____

_____

# CHAPTER 15

# Time & Reputation

I can basically buy anything I want, but I cannot buy time.

—Warren Buffet

Considered one of the most brilliant investors in the world, Warren Buffet is worth well over $75 billion. Interestingly enough, Warren did not come from money. He grew up in a middle-class family in Omaha, Nebraska. Purchasing his first stock at only eleven years old, Warren grew up listening to and watching his father, Howard, run a small stock-brokerage firm. Often he would listen to conversations between his father and other investors.

When Warren was in college, he came across a stock called Geico (worth approximately $40 billion today). Standing out from the crowd, Warren traveled from New York to Washington, DC, to go to Geico's headquarters to do his research. While most stockbrokers and investors will just look at quarterly report earnings and previous stock performance, Warren uses a different tactic.

As a college student, Warren packed up for a trip to DC. Warren got to Geico's headquarters and talked to some leaders of the company—Geico was small enough at the time to do that. Warren was impressed with the company's leadership and decided to invest in the company.

Going the extra mile was something that Warren practiced regularly. It is a characteristic most people do not have because they do not see it as necessary or going the extra mile is simply too cumbersome. With the example Warren gives us, we can better equip ourselves with another skillset the "greats" of our world utilize. Go the extra mile!

## MY STORY

In the same Charlie Rose interview of Bill Gates and Warren Buffet (chapter 14), Bill credited Warren with an invaluable lesson. Warren Buffet pulled out his pocketbook calendar (he is old school), and the audience saw how incredibly careful Warren was with his time. Bill would have every second of his day planned with "busy" items, while Warren would have some days where there was nothing on the schedule. A billionaire with a nonpacked schedule? Hmm, that sounds contradictory.

Warren said he could have anything he wants in life. However, two of the factors he values most are reputation and time. He explained you can spend a lifetime building your reputation, yet it can be dismantled in a moment. Time is something you can never buy or make more of. You have to learn to be conscientious and strategic with your time . . . you only get a limited amount.

When I realized that I did not appreciate and respect my own time, I decided to reorganize my actions. I started by reading a book called *Boundaries* by Dr. Henry Cloud. In this book, I learned how to set healthy boundaries with all my relationships—personal and professional. I learned how to quit saying "Yes" to everything and how to say "No." For me, this was a challenge . . . I am servant-hearted. Assisting people fulfills me, and I am joyful in doing it. However, I also would find myself emotionally and physically drained.

---

Side Note: *Boundaries* is a book I highly recommend, as it will help you continue to be you while helping you understand and develop healthy skills. When you respect your time, you respect yourself. When you respect yourself, you are better prepared. When you are better prepared, you can perform at the level you want and serve those you want to serve.

---

## ACTION STEP 15

Write down what takes up your time in the day. If it is in line with your Aspirations and gets you to your definition of success, keep that time or increase that time. However, if it is not, decrease that time or get rid of it and fill it with something that is in line with your Aspirations and gets you to your definition of success.

## Typical things I do every day

1) _____

2) _____

3) _____

4) _____

5) _____

6) _____

7) _____

8) _____

9) _____

10) _____

## Things I do that are not in line with my aspiration

1) _____

2) _____

3) _____

4) _____

## Things I can fill my time with that are in line with my aspiration

1) _____

2) _____

3) _____

4) _____

---

## PART 4

---

# 1600 Penn Ave: Molding Your Aspirations

# CHAPTER 16

# Bumping into Ivanka Trump

In the end, people should be judged by
their actions, since in the end, it was
actions that defined everyone.

—Nicholas Sparks

Another great that hails from Omaha,
Nebraska, is American novelist, screenwriter, and
philanthropist Nicholas Sparks. Born in 1965,
Nicholas was an exceptional track athlete and an
avid book reader.

Nicholas did not grow up in the 'high life.' He
remembers drinking powdered milk and eating
tons of potatoes. Growing up, he practically never
noticed how poor he was because being poor was

all he knew. However, when he did begin to realize how poor he really was, it did not bother him. He appreciated how he grew up and said he would not change a thing.

As the outgoing high-school-class valedictorian, Nicholas went to Notre Dame, where he and his track relay team would set a school record. While at college, however, Nicholas was injured and was unable to train for his track and field events. Bored that summer, Nicholas gave writing his first book a shot.

Upon finishing his first novel, he was glad it was never published because it was terrible (his words, not mine). After Nicholas wrote the book, he realized something: Even though his work was not quite up to par, he learned he had the ability to finish a novel.

After graduating college with honors in 1988, Sparks met his future wife, Catherine Cote, and a year later they were married. Six weeks after marriage, Nicholas's mother would pass away from a horse-riding accident at the age of forty-seven.

A well-performing pharmaceutical salesman at the time, Nicholas began to get frustrated with his writing career, as he wanted more. He told himself that he would write three more novels, and if nothing got published, he would find something else. In June of 1994, Nicholas began to write *The Notebook* and finished the book in 1995. We know the end of the story: *The Notebook* went on to be the success we know it to be today, selling over 100 million copies, becoming a movie, and grossing over $116 million at the box office.

## MY STORY

In May of 2017, I accomplished one of my goals from chapter 8. I graduated from Freed-Hardeman University on time, and *summa cum laude*. Not only was I able to graduate with the highest honors, but I also was a college athlete competing in track and field and the captain of my university's inaugural track-and-field team.

A few months before I graduated, I was in a business management class and received an email. Reading the email—while my professor was lecturing—I screamed, "Yeah! I got it!"

Interrupted and stunned, my professor asked, "Excuse me, Mr. Gosselin. Is there a problem?" Embarrassed for interrupting, I apologized and sat the remaining fifteen minutes in happiness from the news of the email.

The email I received was a congratulatory message on behalf of the White House Internship Program, affirming my acceptance into the Summer 2017 White House Internship! If you are quick at math, you will realize that 2017 was the inaugural year for the Trump administration. Whether you agree with the administration or not, whether you like Trump or not is not the point.

Serving as an intern for the White House was an opportunity for me to serve you—the American people.

During that monumental summer, I was in the Office of Presidential Correspondence, where we read through *every single* email, snail mail, and phone call that went to the president. It was tedious and monotonous at times; however, I was quick to learn that the federal government does actually serve the American people. (Trust me, I was as skeptical as you.) For example, someone would write to the president asking for help, and the team I was a part of would direct it to the appropriate agency. Sometimes we would get mail a month later from the same people thanking the president for helping their situation. If you are doubtful, I encourage you to write the president. You will be amazed at the assistance you may receive.

One of the humbling honors of interning at the White House was having the opportunity to volunteer for the Congressional Picnic. The Congressional Picnic is an annual gathering of members of Congress and their families held on the South Lawn of the White House. On a typical hot, humid summer day in DC, I helped refill the buffet line with food. Trekking about forty meters from one side of the lawn to the other, while trying to weave through members of Congress with a huge forty-pound cast-iron bowl filled with deep-fried chicken, I finally made it to the buffet table.

I set down the new chicken bowl, picked up the old chicken bowl, and turned to head back to the food preparation tent. Well, midturn, I bumped into a woman. At this point, I was afraid that I just bumped a Congresswoman from Ohio or Virginia, and as I began to apologize, I looked up and had realized I just bumped into Ivanka Trump, the president's daughter! At this point, I was stumbling over my words and afraid I was about to get scolded. You see, up to this point I had not had a personal interaction with the Trumps. I simply knew what the news told me: that the Trumps were not nice.

"I'm so sorry, Mrs. Trump. I didn't mean to bump you," I pleaded.

"Don't worry about it, sweetie. You're doing a great job! I appreciate all of the work you are doing for the White House and American people," she genuinely said.

We would go on to speak for a couple minutes. I would meet Theodore in her arms, Joseph holding her hand, and Arabella tugging at her side. I came to realize how genuine and sincere Ivanka was and how much she truly cared for the American people. I also came to find that this same passion for serving the American people was the case with the entire Trump family and administration. Again, I was just as skeptical as anyone because of the "fake news."

---

Side Note: Be open-minded. Do not allow the media, TV, and social media to be the only place you get information. Be courageous, and think for yourself. Challenge yourself. Be confident and educated on what and why you believe in something.

---

## ACTION STEP 16

Write down something you do not fully understand or a belief that was molded by the media or the people around you. Spend 30 minutes a day for 7 days doing your own research on this topic. It is essential to be OPEN-MINDED! Research from any and all reputable resources, both that support and do not support your current belief. I recommend doing this at least once every 3 months (this is also part of your education from chapter 11).

### First thing I do not fully understand

_____

_____

### 2 media sources that agree with the first thing

1) _____

2) _____

**2 media sources that disagree with first thing**

1) _____

2) _____

**Time of day I will research first thing**

_____

**Second thing I do not fully understand**

_____

**2 media sources that agree with second thing**

1) _____

2) _____

**2 media sources that disagree with second thing**

1) _____

2) _____

# Time of day I will research second thing

_____

_____

# CHAPTER 17

# Become Comfortable with Being Uncomfortable

Comfort kills ambition. Get uncomfortable
and get used to it in your pursuit of your
goals and dreams.

—Robert Kiyosaki

Born in Hawaii in 1947, Robert Kiyosaki started with no money. Although he only made a whopping $25 a month with his first investment, Robert realized that with every single investment—successful or not—he was learning and becoming smarter. Robert went from his first $18,000 property that he 100 percent financed to a $7 million commercial building, which he put $0 down, and it grossed him $30,000 of income every month.

He attributes knowing the difference between these real-estate-investment strategies to his experiencing of a proper financial education, which is not traditionally taught in schools. ("bad debt" vs. "good debt"). Read his book *Rich Dad Poor Dad* to understand that principle better and how he learned it.

Robert is a big proponent of the belief that money is spiritual. Your attitude toward money can determine how much you have–especially if you come from nothing. He says that he makes a lot of money; however, he also gives a lot too. He attributes it to what he sees as a Biblical principle: The more you give, the more you receive. If you want more of something, you have to be willing to give more of something: things you can give vary and can include time, effort, attention, and even money.

Side Note: FOCUS (Follow One Course Until Successful) is another belief Robert has. The book *The One Thing* by Gary Keller and Jay Papasan teaches this belief. When you combine these thought processes and principles taught in both *Rich Dad Poor Dad* and *The One Thing*, you develop a framework to help you become financially successful. Whether you see yourself in business or not, Understanding business and business principles is essential for your success—no matter what it is you pursue. I encourage you to read both books.

## MY STORY

While interning at the White House, I would commute from Upper Marlboro, Maryland, to DC (a twenty-minute drive, forty-minute train ride, and five-minute walk). During this commute, I would read, strategize, and plan how to make the most out of my day, week, and time at the White House. I would arrive at work anywhere between thirty minutes to an hour early, use my lunch breaks as a time to meet fellow interns and people in the administration, and stay late at work if needed. I did not party or go out for dinner— excepting a couple of times for dinner— while interning. Why? Because I wanted to make the most of my time in DC.

I used my experience at the White House to get out of my comfort zone more than I ever had prior. I would introduce myself to people getting lunch in the White House cafeteria area—it can be nerve-racking introducing yourself to a deputy assistant to the president of the United States. I would reach out to "D.C. people" via LinkedIn to see if they would make time for lunch or coffee. You would be surprised how many people are willing to help an aspiring professional wanting to make the most of their time in our nation's capital.

Making myself uncomfortable is something that I strive to do. Becoming comfortable with being uncomfortable is a skill that benefits you greatly. If you are uncomfortable with public speaking, do it more. If you are uncomfortable being a leader, do it more. The more and more you do something, the easier it becomes, and the better you become at it.

After interning at the White House, I traveled up and down the East Coast to attend meetings as a member of a nonprofit's board of directors. (You can read about it in Taya Kyle and Jim DeFelice's book *American Spirit*, profiling thirty individuals who have overcome hardship and done extraordinary things for their communities and nation at large.) Since I could not afford to rent a place and travel for these meetings, I lived out of my car for three months, stayed on family and friends' couches when available, and even would ask strangers for food and gas money when I was running short. If you want to talk about being uncomfortable both mentally and physically, I was doing just that.

## ACTION STEP 17

Write down 5 things that make you uncomfortable. For 67 days straight, make sure you do at least one of those 5 things per day.

**5 things that make me uncomfortable**

1) _____

2) _____

3) _____

4) _____

5) _____

**2 things I can do to make me more comfortable with being uncomfortable with my #11 uncomfortable thing**

1) _____

2) _____

**2 things I can do to make me more comfortable with being uncomfortable with my #2 uncomfortable thing**

1) _____

2) _____

**2 things I can do to make me more comfortable with being uncomfortable with my #3 uncomfortable thing**

1) _____

2) _____

**2 things I can do to make me more comfortable with being uncomfortable with my #4 uncomfortable thing**

1) _____

2) _____

## 2 things I can do to make me more comfortable with being uncomfortable with my #5 uncomfortable thing

1) _____

2) _____

# CHAPTER 18

# Affirmation

Kind words can be short and easy to speak,
but their echoes are truly endless.

—Mother Teresa

Awarded the Nobel Peace Prize—an international award given to the person who best promotes peace, abolition/reduction of standing armies, and fraternity between nations—Mother Teresa was one of the world's foremost leaders of humanitarian efforts. In 1950, the headquarter of the Catholic faith called the Vatican gave Mother Teresa permission to begin her order, the Missionaries of Charity. This organization Aspired to care for the disabled, elderly, and those typically overlooked by society.

A native of what is now Macedonia, Mother Teresa's humanitarian reach eventually expanded from India to the hills of Asia and the plains of Africa. While she was never a biological mother to anyone, Mother Teresa was a mother figure to many. She cared for the weak, the sick, and especially the abandoned. She showed people they were valued and spoke words of affirmation into countless lives.

Mother Teresa was an extraordinary woman who was no stranger to hurt and hardship, having experienced her father passing away at a young age. No matter the struggles she had, Mother Teresa was a fighter and spoke life into all she knew. The power of her efforts and her words is an example we can all look up to.

## MY STORY

While on my Path, I have experienced many hardships and felt the ease of what it would be like to give up (chapter 6 gives more insight). If you want to know a secret I use every day to keep me going, even when I do not want to go anymore, you are reading the right chapter.

When you think of the word *Affirmation*, what is the first thought that pops into your head? Maybe it is a time someone said something nice to you that made you feel good. Perhaps it is something you say in the morning as a reminder of your worth and your value. All this is true; however, I want to break down what "Affirmation" is and, when used correctly, how the definition can significantly increase the odds of Achieving your Aspirations.

Affirmation is fundamentally the process of or being affirmed, reaffirmed, and confirmed in not only who you are but who and what you Aspire to be. I surround myself with people to affirm, reaffirm, and confirm me. Having others speak life, positivity, and affirmation has kept me going. Do I solely rely on it? No. But, it does assist me on my Path.

My affirmation has ranged from the encouragement of incredible people in the President's Leadership Class my freshman year at the University of Oklahoma to the phone calls I will have every other day with a family member or close friend. Although it is important that I receive affirmation, it is equally important to reciprocate affirmation.

---

Side Note: Both self-affirmation (affirmation you tell yourself about your abilities, skills, or goals you possess or will possess) and giving affirmation activate a chemical called dopamine in your brain. Dopamine is associated with the "reward system" of your brain. Not only that, but it wires your brain to be more positive and optimistic. Yes, words truly do matter.

---

## ACTION STEP 18

Remember in chapter 3 when you wrote what success is to you and the characteristics you must embody to achieve that success? Every day make a point to say you possess these characteristics. (Affirm that you are obtaining those characteristics and possess them today.) This should be a part of your morning routine from chapter 4.

If you have not already, be sure to tell or remind the people from chapters 6, 10, and 12 what your definition of success is and characteristics you must possess to achieve that success. Tell them the importance of affirming, reaffirming, and confirming one another in not only who and what they are but who and what they are going to be. Ask them what you can affirm in them.

## 5 characteristics I must possess to obtain my definition of success

(Chapter 3)

1) _____

2) _____

3) _____

4) _____

5) _____

## My 5 people I am grateful for

(Chapter 6)

1) _____

2) _____

3) _____

4) _____

5) _____

## My 5 people who embody a characteristic I strive to obtain

(Chapter 10)

1) _____

2) _____

3) _____

4) _____

5) _____

## My 5 people in my network

(Chapter 12)

1) _____

2) _____

3) _____

4) _____

5) _____

# My 3 people who were out of my network (who are now in)

(Chapter 12)

1) _____

2) _____

3) _____

# CHAPTER 19

# Be Agile

*The thing that made Sam Walton so successful was his ability to be agile and shift on a dime.*

*—Sam Walton's best friend*

Born in 1918 in Kingfisher, Oklahoma (less than two hours from my hometown), Sam Walton created one of the world's largest empires: Walmart. An American entrepreneur, Sam began as a good ol' farm boy from Oklahoma. Sam and his family would later move to Missouri. Having led his high school team to a state championship in Missouri as the quarterback, Sam would later attend the University of Missouri for his education, where he found a particular interest in commerce.

After graduating from college and serving in the United States Army for three years, Sam asked his father for a $20,000 loan to begin his first retail store—a Ben Franklin Variety Store. Running his first retail store is where he learned many of the successful habits that he would later use to build his empire of Walmart. Sam was a humble man and always eager to learn.

Here is a story of Sam's exceptional character while on a business trip to the country of Brazil (Tai Lopez recounts the story in his video course "67 Steps"). On a business trip to Brazil, Sam had some free time and decided to stroll the aisles of a local retail store. Shortly after being in the store, he was accused of being crazy, arrested, and sent to jail, where he had to call the host family he was staying with while in Brazil. Sam's host family asked why the police arrested him and why he was in a Brazilian jail cell; he answered that he was lying in the aisle with a measuring tape to measure the distance between aisles because he wanted to know if what they were doing could have a positive impact on Walmarts in America.

A man worth hundreds of millions of dollars at the time was on the floor of a retail store in Brazil.

Humility.

## MY STORY

There is a psychiatric term called *neuroplasticity*. Neuroplasticity is the brain's ability to rewire, change shape, and develop new neuropathways. For example, shortly after my accident, it was very apparent that my memory was incredibly poor. I could hardly remember what I had for breakfast. Nonetheless, every day I would work on my memory and my abilities to recall. I would use a brain app called Lumosity, with which I would continuously practice cognitive brain exercises, especially memory exercises.

I would practice recall in different ways. For example, when I would go to a restaurant, I would ask the waitress her name and repeat it every time she came to our table, saying things like "Sarah, I greatly appreciate everything you do" or "Sarah, please give my compliments to the chef. The food is delicious."

Not only was this a positive affirmation and something we should all do with wait staff (be kind, respectful, appreciative, and especially, tip), but it allowed me to practice recall.

Side Note: Try this "name tag" exercise sometime and make your server's day. I practice this "name tag' exercise even to this day. My memory performs at a higher level than it ever did before my accident.

Striving to practice Sam Walton's ability to be *agile*, I would put myself in uncomfortable positions that forced me to think quickly and make a quick, intelligent decision. One way I did this was throughout five years of my life: I made sure I did not live in a single area for more than six months. This nomadic lifestyle allowed me to build lifelong friends, "adopt" families throughout the country, and develop the skills of agility.

I had to transform and adapt my businesses; create, mold, and maintain relationships (personal and professional); and adapt to new environments, cultures, and ways of life—some of which I was in the minority. The nomadic lifestyle provided me with the opportunity for growth, learning, and appreciating people who were of different cultures, beliefs, religions, creeds, and ways of life.

I would not change this experience for anything and recommend you open yourself to the learning of people who are "different" than you. You may find yourself realizing you are more alike than you thought. Not as nomadic as I was? Consider a mission trip or volunteering with a group outside of your norm.

# ACTION STEP 19

Remember in chapter 14 you learned to ask yourself if you need to adjust your goals? Make a list of adjustments you need to take on your goals and take action on those adjustments you learned that you need to make. The better you are at adjusting now, the better you become, and the easier it is to adjust down the road.

## Short-term goal #1 adjustments

1) _____

2) _____

## Short-term goal #2 adjustments

1) _____

2) _____

## Short-term goal #3 adjustments

1) _____

2) _____

## Short-term goal #4 adjustments

1) _____

2) _____

## Short-term goal #5 adjustments

1) _____

2) _____

## Medium-term goal #1 adjustments

1) _____

2) _____

## Medium-term goal #2 adjustments

1) _____

2) _____

## Medium-term goal #3 adjustments

1)
_____

2)
_____

## Long-term goal #1 adjustments

1)
_____

2)
_____

# CHAPTER 20

# Walk in Your Faith

The greatest legacy one can pass on
to one's children and grandchildren
is not money or other material things
accumulated in one's life, but rather a
legacy of character and faith.

—Billy Graham

Respected and revered by many, Billy Graham was one of the most prominent evangelists. Born in 1918 in Charlotte, North Carolina, Billy was the first of four children raised on the family's dairy farm. Billy went on to preach to over 215 million people in over 185 countries. He was a considered counselor and confidant to around a dozen United States presidents.

In 1949, Billy began a remarkable journey with the Los Angeles Crusades. Originally scheduled to be a three-week Christian evangelistic campaign, Billy extended the campaign to a full eight weeks. He was impassioned to bring the News of the Gospel and the Message of the Love of Christ to many. In the conclusion of his crusade, he reached over 350,000 people, and over 3,000 people decided to accept Christ as their personal Lord and Savior.

Whether you are a practicing Christian, Muslim, Jew, Buddhist, or any other religion, or choose not to participate in religion, it is unrelated to the fact that Billy Graham set an example we can all follow. Billy Graham believed in who he was and what he was doing. Billy made it apparent that others knew of the mission he was on because he believed it could help them become a better person. Your faith is something that can make or break you. Whatever it is you do or do not believe, make it a point in your life to be consistent, dedicated, and loyal to your faith.

## MY STORY

From a young age, I was always dragged to church by my mother. My mother was adamant about her children going to church. As a kid it was curious growing up in my household because on one side was my mother, a devoted, practicing Christian who reads her Bible every morning at 5 a.m., and on the other side was my agnostic father, who believes there is a greater being, but not necessarily God of the Bible.

Growing up, I did not realize there was an actual difference between Baptist, Methodist, Catholics, and other Christian faiths. I thought we all had the same beliefs, just with different names on the building. It was not until my freshman year of college did I begin to truly understand the differences across denominations of the Christian faith and different religions. And I am still learning today.

As I grow older, I have started to fine-tune and better understand what I believe. Moreover, I am the first to say that I am not a fan of religion. I feel in today's religious world that there is too much focus put on theatrics and not enough on the relationship with the Creator. I consider myself a proud follower of Jesus Christ. I follow the Bible to the best of my ability but also fall short, for I am human. Nonetheless, I am committed to what I believe and am willing to have a conversation with anyone about my faith. My faith keeps me focused, centered, spiritually aligned, and grounded.

Nonetheless, it is essential to respect and to learn about other religions. You do not have to agree with something or someone to respect them (a practice that religion, culture, and politics should have).

---

Side Note: Learning other religions, cultures, and politics helps you grow as a person. It enables you to solidify what and why you believe something while helping you develop the ability to have a calm, collective, productive adult conversation with someone who has different views than you may have. (Again, something that should be practiced more in politics.)

---

Make your faith a priority. Make your culture a priority. Make your character a priority. Make your values a priority. Make being genuine and sincere a priority. Make respect a priority. Trust me; it goes a long way.

## ACTION STEP 20

Take at least 15 minutes per day and focus on your faith. This can be praying, meditating, reading the Bible, etc. Whether you are religious or not, this is a time use to keep you centered and grounded. Answer these questions to help you out.

**What do I believe (what is your faith/ religion)?**

_____

_____

_____

**Why do I believe what I believe?**

_____

_____

_____

**How does what I believe keep me grounded?**

_____

_____

_____

**3 things I am grateful for (speak appreciation in your prayer/meditation)**

1) _____

2) _____

3) _____

**3 things I want to improve (ask for support in your prayer/meditation)**

1) _____

2) _____

3) _____

---
## PART 5
---

# Path to the Presidency: Achieving Your Aspirations

# CHAPTER 21

# Welcome to Failure

Success is not final; failure is not fatal: It is
the courage to continue that counts.

—Winston Churchill

Possibly the most remarkable political leader of the twentieth century, Winston Churchill was born in 1874 in England. Grandson of the seventh Duke of Marlborough and close friends to the ninth Duke and Duchess of Marlborough, Winston was accustomed to spending much time in the Blenheim Palace located in Woodstock, England. Winston grew up with social status and a deep appreciation of heritage.

Winston was a true patriot and understood his people. He won a Nobel Peace Prize, all while he still had his union membership as a bricklayer.

Winston became a politician only after serving on horseback in the front lines of the cavalry. He was continually enriching himself and getting back up, especially after failure.

Winston found himself rising in the ranks of authority in the British Army. Eventually, he would rise to prime minister of the United Kingdom, where Winston would lead the Allied forces during World War II to a victory over the Axis forces.

Even though his father thought Winston would be a failure, Winston rose to power with such charm because of his leadership style. Winston's outlook on politics was not focused on cynicism, which is where many people of his time (as well as today) focused.

---

Side Note: Winston did not focus on partisanship and differences between political parties. He stuck to his convictions and did what he believed was best for his country, not any particular party. As prime minister, Winston Aspired to Unite, not divide.

---

## MY STORY

It was the summer of 2018, where I found myself back home at my parents' house lying in bed. (I always seemed to find myself lying in bed at my parents' home during difficult times in my life.) At this point, I was in my third straight month of severe depression. I was spending about 90 percent of my day just lying in bed—only to get up to eat and use the restroom. My life seemed to be crashing all around me.

I'm sure you may be able to relate to a time where depression crept in. Even with all of the support I had around me, depression was still attacking. My thoughts were not like chapters 2 and 6; this time, I was just content with doing nothing. I was pleased with taking it easy in life and making the smallest effort just to get by.

Some would have said it was acceptable for me to be depressed while knocked down. After all, two of my businesses had just failed, my nonprofit had just failed, and I was failing at two of my closest relationships at the time. I was drained. I put so much effort into my businesses. I spent thousands of dollars and traveled tens of thousands of miles to make my nonprofit successful. Sadly, I was changing my personal Aspirations just to keep those fleeting relationships together.

Finally, around my tenth month of severe depression, I was tired of being tired. I moved a couple times and eventually settled in South Florida for a while. Like Winston, I got back up and kept going. Failure was not fatal. It sucked, but it was not fatal. I was determined to get my feet back under me, get back up, and have the courage to continue. And so, I continued on my Path.

I identified my obstacles (chapter 1), one of which was not having a morning routine (chapter 4). Once again, I surrounded myself with Affirmation (chapter 18). I began to redefine my success (chapter 3). I would set goals (chapter 7) and create actionable steps (chapter 8). I identified new mentors and recalled self-compassion (chapters 10 and 6). I got an "Accountabili-Buddy" (chapter 22). I identified my strengths and weaknesses (chapter 2), which can change over time. Then I wrote my "Referral Testimony" about the time I "shook it off" and "stood up" (chapter 13). I started to implement the things that had once geared me to be successful in the past.

Before I knew it, my life began to turn around. It was not easy, but it was not "hard" either. It was "challenging." I would go on to finish my master's in business administration at Florida Atlantic University in the fall semester of 2020. During the summer of 2020, I applied to become a law student and get my juris doctorate at Arizona State University. Did I get in? No, I did not. However, I did not take that no as a reflection of my ability to be successful. I took it as another opportunity to display courage and continue.

Just like I do little things to improve my memory, I have developed the same habit of doing little things to make improvements in other parts of my life—like the courage to continue. The more you practice something, the better you will become at it. Whether it is negative or positive, you will become better at it.

All the while, I have been running a successful tech startup with a high performing board of advisors and an exceptional executive team. I reimagined my nonprofit's focus during the Covid-19 Pandemic (more on this in chapter 23). Instead of focusing on relationships, I began focusing on being the best version of me I can be.

## ACTION STEP 21

It is a fact that you have not won or accomplished everything in your life. You have failed. There is no getting around it. Write down 3 times you failed and be specific. It can be a test, relationship, sales goal, weight loss, sporting championship, etc. Then, write down why you failed. Was it a lack of dedication? Not enough resources? Not enough time? Poor time management? Lack of support? Poor strategy or lack of strategy? Victim mentality? Once you have those 3 listed and detailed, identify the commonalities of why you failed. Use this as a basis to understand what you commonly resort to that has led to failure. Being aware of this can help you ensure these do not happen in your new goals, Aspirations, and definition of success. We will call this your Red Flags of Failure.

## 3 times I have failed

1) _____

2) _____

3) _____

## Reasons why I failed in #1

1) _____

2) _____

3) _____

## Reasons why I failed in #2

1) _____

2) _____

3) _____

## Reasons why I failed in #3

1) _____

2) _____

3) _____

## 5 common reasons I failed

(what most often caused failure between times 1, 2 & 3)

1) _____

2) _____

3) _____

4) _____

5) _____

## 5 things I can do to avoid my 5 common reasons I failed

(ex: One reason I failed was poor time management, so here I write "keep and maintain a schedule.")

1) _____

2) _____

3) _____

4) _____

5) _____

CHAPTER 22

# Study, Physical Therapy, Pray, Repeat . . .

It always seems impossible until it's done.

—Nelson Mandela

Few people in the history have overcome such oppression as Nelson Mandela and have made the impact he has made. Sworn in as South Africa's first black president, Nelson became president in 1994. However, the journey to achieve this was monumental.

Nelson's efforts led to the multiracial democracy of South Africa that we know today. In 1952 Nelson would go on to form a legal partnership with fellow lawyer and lifelong friend Oliver Tambo. He and Oliver would campaign against the apartheid that eclipsed South Africa. (Apartheid was the political system of South Africa where the white minority ruled the land and crushed the rights of the black majority.)

You see, Great Britain colonized South Africa, so it was owned and run by white people. In fact, before becoming president, Nelson spent nearly thirty years of his life in prison for conspiring to overthrow the government.

Before the courts sentenced him to life in prison in 1982, Nelson Mandela said this in his final plea during his trial:

"It is an ideal which I hope to live for and to see realized. But, my Lord, if needs be, it is an ideal for which I am prepared to die."

The conviction and commitment Nelson had is something we should all have in our Aspirations: be so unwavering that you see no choice but to push on toward your Aspirations; have so much faith that your Aspirations become a part of who you are. We are a better world because of Nelson. We will be a better world because of you. What are you waiting for? What seems to be impossible?

## MY STORY

Like Nicholas Sparks, growing up poor was all I knew, so I did not think much of it. I never envied friends who had nicer houses, cars, and went skiing every year for Christmas. My sense of adventure and curiosity flourished because I never had the newest tech gear or toys. Playing outside, exploring, and using my imagination were things that filled my childhood.

---

Side Note: I understand if you are young, you may not be able to identify with playing outside, but it is something you should try. Put down your iPhone or Xbox controller from time to time and go outside to play. You will see it is not so bad; you will experience significant growth in your life.

---

My parents grew up far poorer than I did. I remember my dad telling me stories of when his family lived in a small apartment in Holyoke, Massachusetts. During the winter, they would all sleep in the living room by the stovepipe that ran through every story of the multilevel, multifamily apartment. This stove pipe would be the source of heat for each family. Not only did they sleep by the stove pipe but they made many meals *on* the stove pipe. He would slice potatoes the thickness of a slice of cheese, put the potato skin on the stove, dash salt and pepper, and "voilà!" they would have dinner.

Not growing up on the East Coast, my mother was from the backwoods of Missouri. Her father left his family (which included my mother, her mother, and her three sisters) when my mother was very young; she has only a few memories of her father. With her father gone, this meant her mother (my grandmother) was rarely home to take care of the kids. As the oldest, my mother had to step up as both the oldest sister and mother to her three sisters. Many times, they would go days without food, and my mom had to find something for them to eat. She would go "hunting" in the woods, find a turtle, bring it back to the house, and "voilà!" turtle soup for dinner.

Growing up without money, I never developed a love for money. As I got older, I have begun to understand and respect money. My future family and many generations after will never have to live the way I did growing up or even the way my parents grew up. My grandparents built a better life for their kids compared to what they had growing up. My parents built a better life for my siblings and I compared to what they had growing up. I am working to build a better life for my future family and generational wealth for the Gosselin families to come. Striving for generational wealth is assisted in not loving money but instead focusing on serving others. It is surrounding myself with incredible mentors and people who believe in me and dedicating my life to learning. Striving to build generational wealth is a possibility for everyone!

"For the LOVE of money is the root of all evil" 1 Tim. 6:10 King James Version

## ACTION STEP 22

From the group of people in chapters 6, 10, and 12, ask 1 or 2 of them to be your "Accountabili-Buddy." Your Accountabili-Buddy is someone(s) who ensures you are following through with your goals and keeps you accountable with your Aspirations. Check in with the person(s) at least once a week. Be honest with them on your progress! You will spend much time with them, so be sure they will have the time to commit, are accessible, and you have a good enough relationship built.

### 2 people to be my Accountabili-Buddy

1) _____

2) _____

### Why did I choose #1 Accountabili-Buddy?

1) _____

2) _____

# Why did I choose #2 Accountabili-Buddy?

1) _____

2) _____

# When During the Week Did My #1 Accountabili-Buddy and I decide to meet?

_____

_____

# How did my #1 Accountabili-Buddy and I decide to meet?

(zoom call, in person, for coffee, mixture of call or coffee depending on distances or other constraints, etc.)

_____

_____

_____

*You can also find the free *Path to the Presidency Workbook* to finish all the action steps at www.PathToThePresidency.com.

# CHAPTER 23

# Build Those Who Built You

Unless someone like you cares a whole
awful lot, nothing is going to get better.
It's not.

—Dr. Suess

Theodor Seuss Geisel (a.k.a. Dr. Seuss) was born in 1904 to Theodor and Henrietta Geisel. Arguably one of the greatest writers of our time, Dr. Seuss had a wild, rebellious side. He began using the pseudonym "Seuss" while in college at Dartmouth because the college banned him from writing for his college. (Dartmouth barred him after he threw a wild party during prohibition.) He added "Dr." because of his father's desire for Seuss to get his doctorate at Oxford. Some have made the comparison that if Dr. Seuss were alive today, he could have been a Platinum rapper like Eminem or Drake.

In his later life, Dr. Seuss was too old to serve on the front lines of World War II, so he decided to instead enlist his talents in producing propaganda for the war. A true patriot, Dr. Seuss was determined to utilize his abilities to help his country win the war. He began to draw cartoons that urged the conservation of resources and to buy United States postage stamps and savings bonds to raise money for the war efforts.

After the war and because of the relationships he developed with US media legends through his war efforts, Dr. Seuss would go on to pen and illustrate some of his most impressive and well-known works, such as *The Cat in the Hat* and *How the Grinch Stole Christmas*. However, his life was not always filled with the same joy he richly brings us through his literary works.

In 1967 his wife passed away from suicide, and after her death, he would find himself struggling with suicidal thoughts himself. He best writes about the struggles and tribulations one will experience in their life through the last book he had ever written, *Oh, the Places You'll Go!*

(1990). This book best describes the struggles and tribulations you will experience throughout your life. From misery to success, he wrote:

> You'll get mixed up, of course,
> As you already know
> You'll get mixed up
> with many strange birds as you go.
> So be sure when you step.
> Step with care and great tact
> And remember that Life's
> a Great Balancing Act.
> Just never forget to be dexterous and deft.
> And *never* mix up your right foot with your left.
> And will you succeed
> Yes, you will
> 99 and ¾ percent guaranteed.

## MY STORY

I am writing this book in the summer and fall of 2020 (a.k.a. "The Year the World Stopped"). During this pandemic, I have seen marriages strengthen, and marriages fall. I have seen wealth created and wealth destroyed. I have seen communities rising together to fight for a better future, and I have seen cities shut down and destroyed. I have seen the best in people and the worst in people. With many stuck at home, 2020 has been an opportunity for all of us to reflect, strategize, and improve.

In early March, many schools began to shut down. Many hospitals began to operate at capacity (and sometimes fuller). The pandemic forced many mom-and-pop businesses and churches to close— some indefinitely. With family and community being important to me, my mind went straight to my hometown of Burlington, Oklahoma. I wanted to help; I wanted to be there for the community that helped mold me into who I am today.

In early May, I decided to do something about it. I formed a nonprofit 501(c)(3) organization called The Empowering B.A.C.K. Foundation (**B**urlington, OK; **A**lva, OK; **C**herokee, OK; and

**K**iowa, KS). Each of these incredible communities played a role in my upbringing.

We utilized resources to donate masks to the hospital systems in each of these towns. Then we created a scholarship fund so that every high-school senior in those four towns would have a scholarship. These scholarships would help to financially support the students for college, a technical degree, or any decision they made, as long as it pushed them to what they wanted to pursue. (To receive the scholarship, you had to handwrite a thank-you letter to someone who has positively impacted you¬—which sounds a little like chapter 6?) Lastly, faith is a significant cornerstone of where I am from, so our foundation donated masks to all thirty-two churches in those communities.

---

Side Note: Times of stress and tribulation should not bring out the worst in people; it should bring the best. Never forget where you come from and who Molded you and is Molding you to who you are becoming.

---

Coming from a great community, we were not the only organization that helped these communities during this time; nonetheless, it was an honor to be a part of the effort.

## ACTION STEP 23

Write down 3 groups, organizations, or communities that have helped you get to where you are today. Find ways to help them now and strategize how to help them in the future. (Remember also to be protective of your time.) Not sure what they need? Ask them. This might help you with chapter 17's task for the day.

### 3 groups, organizations, or communities (GOC) who helped mold me

1) 
_____

2) 
_____

3) 
_____

### Contact at GOC #1

_____

MY PATH to the PRESIDENCY

**Contact at GOC #2**

_____

**Contact at GOC #3**

_____

**What can I do to help GOC #1?**

_____

**What can I do to help GOC #2?**

_____

**What can I do to help GOC #3?**

_____

# CHAPTER 24

# Remove "Can't" from Your Vocabulary

Whether you think you can, or you think
you can't—you're right.

—Henry Ford

Told he would not last six months in business, Henry Ford went on to be one of the wealthiest people of his time. From a young age, Henry showed interest in engineering, and throughout his childhood and teen years, he would take engineering and manufacturing internships every chance he could get.

In his spare time, he built the "quadricycle," which put two bicycles together, a seat and steering wheel in the middle, and a gasoline engine—the first primitive car he built. While he was not the first to make a car, Henry was the first to bring the assembly line to the dawn of the car manufacturing era.

At his peak, Henry had an estimated wealth in today's money of over $180 billion. Henry Ford had plenty of failures before his success, but he never gave up. When he first told people he wanted to mass manufacture quality cars via his "assembly line" idea, people would laugh at him and mocked him, with many saying it was impossible. It would not be long after that the Model T would come to the streets of America and the world via his assembly-line idea.

Henry stressed quality in everything he did. He would not go into a business unless he was confident he could do it with quality. He saw so many entrepreneurs of his time that failed because they did not focus on quality or the consumer (something that still happens to this day).

Henry also stressed the importance of building an incredible team. He would hire people, not looking at their past, but instead looking at whether or not they were willing to work. He believed that every person had good in them, and they just needed an opportunity to prove it. Henry Ford's leadership set the foundation for the Ford Motor Company to grow into the automotive industry leader it is today.

## MY STORY

Much like the thesis of this book—"Life is not *Hard*, it is Challenging"—there is another word that is much like hard. It, too, has psychological and unconscious obstacles you may not be aware of. Henry Ford knew the word. The word is *can't*, and when used incorrectly, it can be detrimental to your success. The term *can't* can be indicative of whether or not someone will accomplish what they set out to do.

Having delivered my message to tens of thousands of people, I always found the idea of *can't* to be one of the critical elements that serve as a foundation for my message. Whether I am speaking at a commencement ceremony for a high school, a Freshman Orientation Week for a university, or keynote speaking at a leadership camp, I portray the impact *can't* has on our lives.

When I tell stories on stage (my stage name is the Aspirational Storyteller), I try rationalizing with my audience what the word *can't* does to your unconscious mind and how to reframe your thoughts. For example, instead of saying,

"I can't be a varsity sports player,"

"I can't graduate college with all As and Bs,"

"I can't build a successful multimillion-dollar business,"

say something like this:

"Right now, I have not acquired the skills to play on the varsity team; however, I am going to practice diligently thirty extra minutes a day until I do."

Or say,

"Finishing college with all As and Bs seems impossible. Nonetheless, I am going to get tutoring at least three times a week, take notes during class, and review my notes right after class."

---

Side Note: It is scientifically proven, reviewing notes right after class decreases the time needed to study before a test.

---

Also, when a venture fails, just think that

"Although I have had many businesses fail in the past, I will strategize, have a great work ethic, surround myself with mentors, and have the right team to build a multimillion-dollar business."

Understandingly, the second approach is much more time consuming and takes more brainpower than just to say, "I can't . . ." However, by excluding the word *can't* and replacing it with a solution to your problem, you create new neuropathways (a.k.a. neuroplasticity). You not only negate *can't* but also identify the solution and develop an action plan to solve the solution.

Doing this is NOT easy, but it's not HARD either!

## ACTION STEP 24

Every time you say "can't," write down why you said it and in what context. That night, right before you go to bed, restate your statement without "can't" as you learned above.

**1st can't statement**

_____

_____

**1st can't statement reworded without** *can't*

_____

_____

_____

**2nd can't statement**

_____

_____

**2nd can't statement reworded without** *can't*

_____

_____

_____

**3rd can't statement**

_____

_____

**3rd can't statement reworded without** *can't*

_____

_____

_____

# CHAPTER 25

# Start Today

People often tell me I could be a great man.
I'd rather be a good man.

—John F. Kennedy Jr.

"Ask not what your country can do for you, but what you can do for your country." These are the words spoken by 35th President of the United States, John F. Kennedy (JFK).

JFK was the beloved father of John F. Kennedy Jr., who was born after his father won the presidential election for the United States of America in 1960. When John was only three years old, a sniper assassinated President Kennedy. One of the world's first memories of young John was of him saluting his father's coffin at the president's memorial service.

John was a man who marched to his own beat. John did not want to do what everyone thought he should do. He was well aware of himself and knew he was perfectly positioned to be a great man—everyone expected it of him. John had the right family, enough money, and a good upbringing. People get into politics for either money, power, or fame. He had all three when he was born. Although positioned well, he decided to make his focus on not being a great man but a good man. After realizing a lot of "great men" really were not good men at home, John was determined to be a good man.

He wanted to be the best husband he could to his wife, Carolyn. He wanted to be the best brother he could to his siblings. He wanted to be the best son he could be to his parents. John—a man who had it all—wanted to focus on being a good man.

In his mother's last letter before she passed, Jackie Kennedy wrote, "YOU, especially have a place in history." After her passing, John started a magazine called George where his focus was to be organic, to bring sensibility to politics, and to take the "dryness" out of politics by merging politics and pop culture.

MY PATH to the PRESIDENCY

It is no doubt that John was a presidential hopeful—many people, even to this day, wish that to be. However, in 1996 his plane went missing. John will forever go down in history as a man who many looked up to, but more importantly, a good man.

## OUR STORY

Start today.

It is okay to fail. We are in this together.

Have self-compassion.

Understand the differences between motivation, inspiration, and Aspiration.

Always understand Affirmation and the importance of surrounding yourself with it and giving it.

Always strategize, plan, and surround yourself with mentors.

Aspire and chase after your goals with relentless forward motion. Before you know it, you will have gone further than you ever thought you could go. Further than your friends and family thought you could go. In some cases, further than your doctors thought you could go.

Your Friend,

Brandon Gosselin #BG2032 #UNITED

Side Note: By the end of this book, I hope you feel motivated and inspired, but more importantly, I hope you believe you have the tools to begin to lay the foundation for what you Aspire to be and do. Remember, life is not going to be easy, but "Life is not *Hard*" either. And along your Path, do not forget to be a good person.

## ACTION STEP 25

You now have an action plan to achieve your Aspirations. Below write how you will succeed in Achieving your Aspirations. If you have access to the Internet and a printer, go to www. PathToThePresidency.com. You will find the FREE *Path to the Presidency Workbook*. Print out all of the sheets and fill them out by hand. (Fill out by hand because there is a more significant positive subconscious effect that happens when you handwrite compared to typing.) Staple them together in order or put them in a binder. THESE ACTIONS STEPS ARE YOUR Aspirational Action Plan. Trust me; if someone as simple as me can overcome and achieve what I have so far, I can only imagine the incredible things you are going to do.

**Write "I believe I will succeed in Achieving [insert Aspiration]" from chapter 7. Do this 5 times.**

1) _____

_____

_____

2) _____

_____

_____

3) _____

_____

_____

4) _____

_____

_____

5) _____

_____

_____

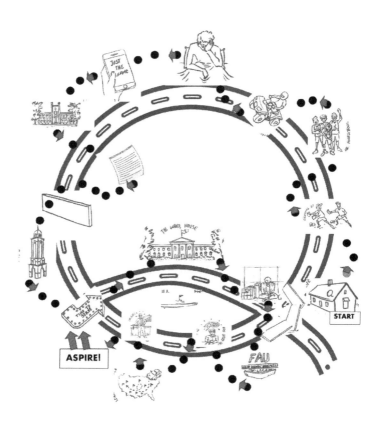

## One Last Thing, One Last Action Step

In closing, I humbly request that you consider being my Accountabili-Buddy. As I Aspire to understand the American people and what it is truly like to be American, I will need your help. As you know, our incredible country is richly and wonderfully diverse. I Aspire to understand why we act, think, and do what we do as individuals and as a society. I Aspire to understand different cultures, religions, creeds, and people.

My Aspiration is to be on the forefront of getting us to be the UNITED States of America. What matters most is we Aspire together, we respectfully set aside our differences, and we ALL strive to UNDERSTAND and UNITE with one another.

Right now I am currently unable (not using "can't") to truly understand everyone's perspective to effectively be on the forefront of leading us to the UNITED States of America. But with your help, I believe we can. Yes, I have been homeless, evicted, and lived paycheck to paycheck. I have lived in the minority of both race and religion. I have lived in the poorest communities to the most affluent. However, I have much to learn. Thus, I propose the Final Action Step.

## FINAL ACTION STEP

Tell me about you. Let me know your struggles, your experiences, your perspectives, your beliefs, how you have been oppressed, and how you believe our country should be led to UNITE and UNDERTAND each other. This is something that will take all of us to accomplish. This is something that can be accomplished with your help.

You can create a video, write a letter, make a recording, or any way you would like to share this final action step. Yes, I will never truly understand what it is like to live in your shoes, but I sincerely want to know how I can best represent YOU.

Go to our website to learn the best way to submit your Final Action Step.

(www.PathToThePresidency.com)

**About You**

_____

_____

_____

## Your Struggles

_____

_____

_____

## Your Experiences

_____

_____

_____

## Your Perspectives

_____

_____

_____

## Your Beliefs

_____

_____

## Your Oppressions

_____

_____

_____

## How you think we can UNITE and UNDERSTAND

_____

_____

_____

_____

_____

ency

## Notes

_____

_____

_____

_____

_____

_____

_____

_____

_____

_____

_____

_____

_____

- 235 -

## Notes

Made in the USA
Columbia, SC
19 May 2023

16290051R00150